KT-415-801

CHINA PAINTING
Projects
AROUND THE WORLD

CHINA PAINTING
Projects
AROUND THE WORLD

SHEILA SOUTHWELL

BLANDFORD

Blandford

an imprint of
Cassell
Villiers House, 41/47 Strand
London WC2N 5JE

First published 1991

British Library Cataloguing in Publication Data
Southwell, Sheila
  China painting around the world.
  1. Pottery & porcelain. Painting
  I. Title
  738.15

ISBN 0–7137–2151–0

Distributed in the United States by
Sterling Publishing Co, Inc,
387 Park Avenue South, New York, NY 10016–2880

Distributed in Australia by
Capricorn Link (Australia) Pty Ltd
PO Box 665, Lane Cove, NSW 2066

Typeset in Monotype Plantin by
August Filmsetting, Haydock, St Helens
Printed and bound in Spain by Graficromo

This book is dedicated to our two sons
Neil and Tim
who have watched my hobby develop into a full-time profession

Contents

Acknowledgements

My thanks go to the following
for their help in the research of this book

Mary Moorcroft – Royal Doulton
Gladstone Pottery Museum – Stoke on Trent
Mavis Quartermain – Australia
Victoria and Albert Museum – London
John Cushion – Ex Senior Research Assistant V & A
Peter Broadbridge – LAPADA
Geoffrey Godden – Worthing
Eskenazi Gallery – London
L. Griffin – Clarice Cliff Collectors Club
Somlak Balankura – Bangkok
Britta Gertsen – Royal Copenhagen Porcelain

Special thanks to my husband Alan,
who photographed all my pieces for this book.

Preface

When you don't know how, painting is easy.
When you do know, it's a different matter.

Edgar Degas
1834–1917

When asked by my publishers to write a third book I had little difficulty deciding the theme. The art of china painting is truly international and we all enjoy seeing what other countries have to offer, so the subject seemed obvious – a trip around the world, stopping along the way to sample the flavours of other countries whose porcelain we have long admired. Through these pages we will visit Europe, Asia, Australia and the USA.

In this book I will not be discussing 'how to do it' techniques as these have already been fully covered in my previous two books. I will be concentrating more on styles of decoration. Each chapter will contain designs characteristic of a featured country, showing the flora or fauna, and either a visit to a famous porcelain factory or an in-depth look at a particular type of ceramic from that country. Each design will have a step-by-step project for you to follow, so pick up your brushes and come with me on my magic carpet around the world.

Happy Painting

Sheila Southwell

Painter and Poet

Fill my palette with green and brown
For sturdy trunk and leafy crown.
The morning light has tipped with gold
The fresh young growth, 'though the root is old;
Born of the earth, the rain and the sun,
The soul of the tree and I are one.
How shall I paint you, tree, my brother?
Kin with the earth and with each other.

Shades of violet and shades of blue –
Colour of sky and distant view;
Brilliant blue of a summer day –
Gathering storm clouds, white and grey;
Roseate hues of the setting sun
Where earth meets sky, and they melt in one.
How shall I paint you, sky, my brother?
Kin with the earth and with each other.

Sapphire shades of the open sea,
Home of the seabird wheeling free;
Blue and green of the sheltered bay;
Salt crisp white of the breaking spray;
Waves that break on the rocky shore –
Break, and retreat, and return once more.
How shall I paint you, sea, my brother?
Kin with the earth as father and mother.

Purple mountain and endless plain;
Rush of wind and the falling rain;
Soft wet earth that follows the flood;
Song of a bird, and quickening bud;
Things of the earth, all fair and free,
That waken the wonder and rapture in me.
How can I paint them, earth, our mother?
Kin with us all and each with other.

I have no colour for wind on the plain.
I cannot paint the scent of rain.
The brush will draw what the eye can see –
But not the bond that enraptures me.
I am the wind, I am the tree,
I am the bird, the sky and the sea.
All that is, is sister and brother,
Kin with the earth and with each other.

Mavis Quartermaine, Kalgoorlie, Australia

1. Basic Principles

Some leaves, showing the diversity of their shapes

Before we start our journey there are a few basic art principles to be taken on board. It is not sufficient just to be able to paint a pretty design – some rules must be observed, such as light, harmony and balance, if you are to achieve a well-designed and executed painting. All too often I see pieces painted with little or no thought being given to light and shade and with attention focused on no particular part of the design. Sometimes students will show me a piece which they consider to be finished, but with a little more work and thought could be improved beyond recognition. When shown just a few added accents here and there, they find the difference unbelievable. It is usually at times like this that you hear the phrase 'magic brush' whispered about. It is not a magic brush your teacher is using – just applied knowledge and possibly years of experience! I have illustrated some of the main faults in the following paragraphs – see if you are guilty of any of them.

Here are a few fundamental useful points. It is easy to become too entrenched in the principles of art and this can be confusing to students if, like myself, they have received no art training. I will therefore try to find the happy medium and pick out the main things of which to be aware, and if you follow these your painting can only improve.

Colour

A comprehensive study of colour can become extremely complex, as it will cover four basic areas of specialized science – physics, chemistry, psychology and physiology – and if studied too deeply can confuse and discourage the painter whose main interest is to produce an attractive design. My main intention is to explore, on a simple level, how colours work together and in harmony.

Three Dimensions of Colour

HIV or hue, intensity, value. If you were asked to differentiate between the three colours on p. 14 you would probably say that one is red and that the other two are green. If pressed you might say that one green is light and one is dark. If further pressed you might indicate that one green is a yellow green and one is a blue green. This simple analysis describes the characteristics of colours, and is commonly known as the three dimensions of colour. Try to keep these dimensions in your mind when you are painting.

Hue

The most obvious dimension which identifies a colour by its name is the hue – yellow, red, blue and all colours belong to a 'hue family'. We talk about purples, reds, blues etc., knowing that these colours can incorporate many shades.

Intensity

The second dimension is the intensity of the hue, the brightness or the dullness. Colours containing more of the original hue are described as being more intense or darker.

Value

The third dimension, known as value, indicates the lightness or darkness of a colour in its relation to white or black. A light colour such as yellow is higher in value because of its close proximity to white. Blue is closer to black and so it is lower in value. A good way to remember all this is to imagine that white is the most 'expensive' colour so it is highest in value, and the closer any colour is to white the 'higher' is its value. Black is at the lower end of the scale, and so colours closer to it are 'lower' in value, i.e. pale blue is higher in value than dark blue.

There is no colour without light. A full spectrum of colours can be seen in a rainbow, as it can when light passes through a prism. The range of colours is shown on the colour wheel. Joseph Addison, the eighteenth-century essayist, said, 'Among the several kinds of beauty, the eye takes most delight in colour.' Use the colour wheel to decide which colours to use in your backgrounds.

Primary Colours: *Red, Yellow, Blue*

These are colours which cannot be made out of any other colours, but which when combined in various proportions with each other can make many other colours.

Complementary Colours

These are colours which are opposite each other on the colour wheel and which complement each other when used together. If you are using yellow flowers as your main subject, the perfect background is violet. An obvious complement to red is green – think of those lovely Christmas colours. To make a complementary grey use two colours opposite each other mixed together.

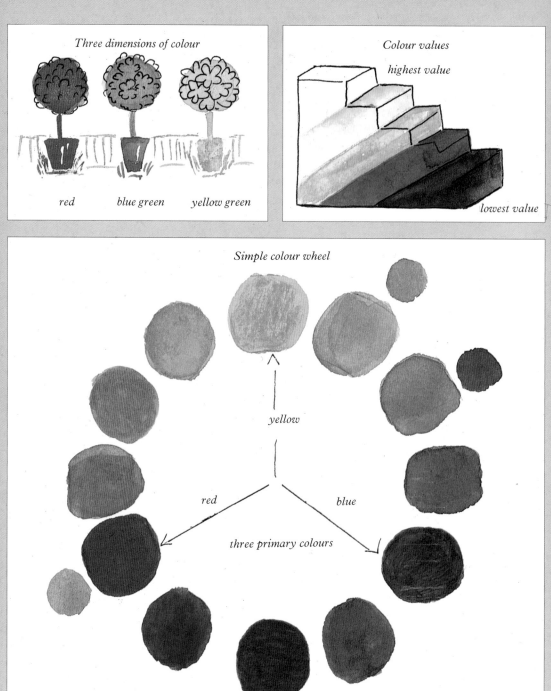

Three dimensions of colour

red   blue green   yellow green

Colour values

highest value

lowest value

Simple colour wheel

yellow

red   *blue*

three primary colours

Complementary colours are opposite on the wheel and when mixed together form a sympathetic grey

Primary colours

Colour balance

Complementary colours

Warm and cool colours

The distant hills in a landscape recede when painted paler and cooler against a dark, sharp foreground

A pale blue vase – or dark blue curtains?

Secondary Colours

These are the colours placed between the primary colours – greens, violets, oranges.

Tertiary Intermediate Colours

These additional hues, which fall between the primary and secondary colours, can be made by mixing the adjoining primary and secondary colours.

Colour Harmony

Harmony is the result of a balanced relationship between chosen colours, and a harmonious colour scheme relies on a pleasing balance of hues. Try to achieve reasonable moderation in colour combinations as extremes may be disturbing. However, do not be too moderate or your painting will be uninteresting; use your discretion and try to achieve a happy medium. Monochromatic harmony is perhaps the easiest to achieve; by using different values of the same colour, interesting effects can result. What you are striving for is a 'harmonious whole'.

Colour Balance

Your aim is to produce a well-balanced painting, and not one in which any particular part of the design dominates. Colour contrast can be an important factor. Imagine a pair of scales with dark blue on one side and yellow on the other; the blue, of course, will look heavier in value and be more dominant. Study your completed piece: does it look unbalanced? If it does, would a little more colour help? Hold the piece up to a mirror. Does one area 'pull your focus'? If so, adjust the colour on the appropriate section.

How much of the area should you cover with colour and how much leave blank? An ideal balance in a naturalistic design is two-thirds design and one-third negative space. However, too little is better than too much. You can always add more later.

Colour Temperature

Colour is used to indicate warmth or coolness. To create a warm feeling, choose shades of red, pink, orange and peach. To create a cooler effect, use blues, greens and mauves etc. If you place two reds together and add a little blue to one of them, you will create a cooler shade of red.

Colour Mixing

Most china painting pigments are fully intermixable, and from a fairly limited palette you can obtain many lovely colours. A great deal of experimenting is the best way to find out how your colours work together; don't forget to keep a record of your tests for future reference. Colours containing cadium and selenium may not be mixed with other colours. Personally I prefer lots of colours, but I have a hard core of favourites which I am never without. These include yellow-red, yellow-brown, chartreuse, antique green, dark ruby, rose pink and malachite blue. A good deep black is also useful. Flesh colours in portraits often present problems, but there are now several lovely collections of portrait colours available from suppliers. Flesh tones vary according to the subject's racial origins, and often several colours will need to be mixed to obtain the correct shade. A good basic colour is ivory, to which other colours may be added. Some which I find useful are pale yellow red, portrait grey, flesh pink and peach. Avoid using bright reds and pinks. The hands, feet, ears and nose etc. are always darker than the adjacent areas because blood is more concentrated in these parts. Body areas exposed to the elements are always redder than areas protected by clothing.

If no basic knowledge of colour is employed, even a monochromatic scheme can create problems. Look at the bottom right picture on p. 15 – is this a light blue vase on a dark blue background, or is it a light blue background behind dark blue curtains? See what I mean?

Leaves: A Perennial Problem

If china painters were asked to name the one aspect of their work which bothered them most, the majority would answer 'leaves'. Leaves are an important feature in any design, and badly painted foliage can ruin what would otherwise be a lovely piece of work. Here are some of the most common faults.

Overworking

This is the most frequent fault I have found. If leaves are con-

Leaves painted in the Rookwood style

stantly worked over they will lose most of their freshness and will look muddy and dead. On the first fire it is important not to keep fiddling with a lot of itty-bitty brush strokes. Also on the first firing the colours should be kept light and clean. Use either a chartreuse or a light yellow-green – other shades may be introduced on the next and subsequent fires. Do not paint over the entire leaf on the first fire, but leave some good strong highlights. I find many students think that the whole leaf must be covered each time they paint, and the result is usually dull and lifeless-looking, particularly if they use the same dull green each time.

Background

Another fault I come across regularly is painting the background the same shade of green as the leaves. This again leads to a dull-looking piece with no colour contrast. Aim to get several tones of colour into your foliage.

Light and Shade

If you study a spray of leaves you will notice that some leaves catch the light and others are in shadow; then look through half-closed eyes and you will see this effect more clearly. The high-lighted leaves will be higher in value (closer to white, remember) than the ones in the shade. Another point to note is that, where the leaves turn back, the area which is folded over will be paler, where it catches the light, than the parts shaded by the turnback. Learn to think about light and shade – I see leaves all the time where the turned back area has been painted darker than the shaded part. This of course is impossible in nature, and only proves that the student has not given any thought to what he or she was painting. As I mentioned earlier, I have had no formal art training – but I was lucky to have a teacher who made me stop and look, and this has been good advice.

One of the most boring plates I have ever seen was one where all the flowers were the same shade of pink and the leaves all a middle value of green. The whole design was devoid of any shading whatsoever, but with a few darks tucked in the plate was transformed – to the amazement of the student. No matter how well your brushwork is executed, if there is no light and shade there is no interest. At exhibitions I see plates which look totally unfinished, and I long to tell the painter responsible to add more strong background colours. Even the most delicate design must have light and shade.

I believe the problem arises because students often do not know what to do after the initial firing, which was probably quite successful. Do not be afraid to try adding some darks such as black green or American beauty, or a little of both mixed together, for a lovely warm, dark shade. Shadow leaves are beautiful painted with grey and American beauty mixed on your brush. Another nice shadow-leaf colour is antique green.

Study the paintings of leaves in the picture on p. 11 and you will see what I mean. Silk leaves are excellent for study purposes; look at them and turn them about, with twists and turnbacks here and there, and you will soon get to grips with them. I use a lot of silk flowers for study as the ones made these days are excellent and often cannot be distinguished from the real thing in flower arrangements. They also have the advantage of staying where you place them, unlike real flowers and leaves.

Stems

Look how the leaves are joined to their stalks or stems, how they sit behind the flowers, and how they connect with the flowers and leaves – do they join the stem in pairs or singly? If you have several flowers in your design make sure the leaves overlap some of the flowers. In nature you would not see the whole of every flower; some of them would be shaded by foliage.

Botanical Accuracy

Do not be guilty of putting the wrong leaf with your flower. This was an early mistake I made – I was mortified at an exhibition of classwork when a visitor said loudly, 'Those aren't proper violet leaves, they don't grow like that'. Food for thought!

Simplicity of Brush Strokes

Lastly, if you learn to use your brushes correctly a leaf can be made with just a few strokes. Practice here is important.

Advanced Techniques

Whilst in the Preface at the beginning of the book I stated that I didn't intend to go into detail about different techniques, there are three which deserve explanation as, in my opinion, they are the most difficult decorating techniques to master. They are groundlaying, raised enamel and raised paste and are done as follows.

Groundlaying

Groundlaying is a method of obtaining a deep, opaque background colour in just one firing, which is often used with reserved panels decorated with flowes or scenes, etc. It is the most difficult technique in my opinion and will take plenty of practice to produce a good piece. As loose powdered paint is used in larger quantities A FACE MASK MUST BE WORN for safety.

The powder should be sieved through two layers of nylon hose as there must be no small lumps of colour to ruin the effect. The area to be groundlaid is then painted with groundlaying oil (it helps to add a small quantity of the powdered colour, which will enable you to see where you have painted), making sure the complete area is covered. Then, using a silk pad, go over the oiled area with a smooth padding movement until the oil is completely even, with only a small amount left on the china. The pad will make a 'sucking' sound when the area is sufficiently padded. Using a ball of cotton wool, take up a large quantity of the sieved colour and gently apply it to the oiled area with a rolling motion: the loose cotton wool must not be allowed to come into contact with the oil, so there must be a good layer of powdered colour between the cotton wool and the china.

When the complete area is covered, gently remove the surplus colour, using a soft blending brush. The piece should now have the appearance of suede leather with no white patches of china showing through. The idea is to get an even layer of powder all over the piece – if you get more colour in one area than another it is no good and must be done again (I told you it was difficult!). Be extra careful when placing the pot in the kiln that you do not allow it to touch anything and don't scratch it with your finger nail. Fire very hot. On removal from the kiln the piece should have a beautiful dark, glossy, evenly-coloured background. If there are lighter areas showing through, you have not done it correctly!

Raised Paste and Raised Enamels

These are two completely different things and often confuse china painters. They are both used to add another dimension to your work and are made to stand out in relief from the body of the china and porcelain. A good way of remembering which is which is to bear in mind that raised paste powder is yellow and is used with gold, while raised enamel powder is white and used alone or with coloured enamels. They are often called relief paste or relief enamels. Special oils are available for use with these powders and give marvellous results if correctly mixed. The same oil is used for both and thinned with water, also the brush used is cleaned with water not turps. Alternatively, you can mix with fat oil and thin with pure turpentine to the correct consistency. It is also possible to purchase ready-mixed paste/enamels in small jars.

Raised Enamel

Mix the white powder with sufficient relief oil to make a crumbly texture and then thin with water till the enamel is like thick cream. Then apply to your design, using a fine pointed brush. You should practise until you can make little scrolls and dots with nice clean edges. If the edges are fuzzy you must wipe it all off and start again. Practice makes perfect – there are no shortcuts to this one. If you would like coloured scrolls you can mix just a little of your onglaze colour with the prepared enamel, but remember that it will fire darker. Fire at 760°C. The enamel will flow onto the china better if it is picked up in small globules on the brush and 'pulled' into the desired shape on the china. The enamel should be allowed to dry for several hours before firing. If after firing it has blistered, you have used too much oil. Little can be done to rectify this except to apply more enamel and re-fire. After firing do not rub your fingers over the raised work as this is often sharp and may cut your fingers.

Raised Paste

This is reserved for use with burnishing gold and is hardly ever used for anything else. It is mixed and applied in exactly the same way as the raised enamel, bearing in mind that it is to be covered with burnishing gold after firing. Bright gold is NEVER used over raised paste and if you try the results will be disappointing and you will waste your gold. After firing the raised paste, you must very carefully cover it with burnishing gold using a fine brush, making sure that you only cover the paste and not the surrounding china. There is no doubt that this, when well done, is the epitome of fine art. Only attempt this when you know you are proficient with raised enamels or you will only waste your precious and expensive gold. Fire the gilding at approximately 760°C and burnish after firing. Raised paste/gilding should be the last process to be done on a prestige piece. Practise this technique by using raised enamels, then after firing paint over with a dark lustre and examine the piece with a magnifying glass. Only when you can cover the enamel exactly are you ready to use the gilding procedure.

2. England

A potbank yard, Stoke on Trent, c.1845

I decided to start our journey in England with a visit to north Staffordshire, the heart of the British china industry and known the world over as the home of bone china. In the area called 'The Potteries' there were large deposits of fuel with which to fire the kilns. This is why the area was popular with potters centuries ago – not because of the deposits of china clay, which are to be found elsewhere. The Potteries contain many ceramic companies large and small and most of the ware made is bone china, unlike factories on the Continent which make mostly porcelain. Before discussing some important English china factories I will enlarge a little on some of the basic distinctions between different kinds of ceramics.

Ceramic Terms

China

This is a generic term used originally to distinguish Chinese porcelain from that of the European potters, which was heavier and thicker. Confusingly, it became associated with all porcelain and pottery, and is now often used in broad terms by the layman to describe any type of ceramic.

Porcelain

This is a word correctly used to describe hard paste porcelain, often called true porcelain. It is made of kaolin (china clay) and feldspar (aluminium silicate) and the formula has been known to the Chinese for about 1200 years, but because they kept their secret so well it was not until 1708 that it was first made in Europe at what was shortly to become the Meissen factory in Germany. When broken, hard paste porcelain has a very hard edge with the clay tightly packed. It does not absorb stains.

Soft paste porcelain was an imitation of hard paste, manufactured in Europe in the seventeenth century out of various components, such as white clay and ground glass, in an attempt to imitate Chinese porcelain. When broken it has a more open texture which absorbs stains and acids; it also crumbles on breaking. My work as a ceramics restorer brings me many pieces to repair and I can study these at will, but it is interesting to note the number of clients who telephone me to say they have broken a piece of porcelain – only for me to discover on examination that the piece is made from earthenware or pottery and that the broken edges have crumbled badly and lost slivers of glaze. This rarely happens with porcelain of the hard paste variety.

Bone China

This is made by mixing bone ash with a clay mixture made from china clay and china stone, and a small proportion of alkalis. Bone china was perfected by Josiah Spode in about 1800, and can be distinguished from porcelain by its whiteness and high glaze. The china painter's enamel colours are more readily absorbed into the glaze of bone china than porcelain, because of the softer body of the ware.

Many china painters outside Britain, who are not familiar with bone china, think that painting on this body is difficult. This is not so, providing that the china is of good quality and has not been stored in a damp place. I have had the odd piece which has developed black mildew spots in the firing – but so few that it is hardly worth mentioning. However, if this happens to you just fire the piece at a very high temperature and the spots will often disappear. Certainly the beautiful glaze on bone china will delight you.

One thing you must never do with bone china is to allow it to touch other pieces during the firing process – because of the softness of the glaze, the pieces will fuse together.

Pieces of porcelain, on the other hand, if carefully stacked, will not stick together; i.e., lidded boxes may be fired with the lids on and plates may be stacked together.

Pottery

This denotes anything made from clay and is used for all types of ware. It is an opaque and soft glazed ware, usually decorated under the glaze.

Earthenware

This is also opaque and made from clay fired between 800 and 1200°C. It does not vitrify (forms its own surface glaze) and often an opaque glaze is added. Tiles and flowerpots are made from earthenware, as is some tableware. Salt-glazed earthenware, with its attractive 'orange peel' effect, was the poor man's alternative to porcelain in the eighteenth century.

Stoneware

This is earthenware fired at temperatures exceeding 1200°C, at which it vitrifies and therefore does not need additional glazing.

Selected Early English Factories

Chelsea

The anchor was a mark used by the Chelsea factory after 1749. At various periods it was painted in different colours, either red, purple, blue or gold

Founded about 1745 and possibly the oldest china factory in Britain. Delicate copies of Meissen figurines, large tureens and delicate snuffboxes were popular items. Chelsea dinner services based on the designs of Sèvres and Vincennes were outstanding.

Worcester

Founded 1751. This factory was established by a consortium including Dr Wall, who gave his name to the greatest period of Worcester. Porcelain painted in underglaze blue with Chinese designs was followed by painted landscapes of local scenes and flora and fauna. Much later, in the present century, Dorothy Doughty was to become famous for her beautifully modelled birds and Doris Lindner for her horses. Royal Worcester is famous also for its hand-painted fruit designs and landscapes with Highland cattle, of which the greatest exponent was John Stinton. Today quantities of dinnerware are produced.

This Royal Worcester mark was first used in 1852 in the form of a circle without a crown. The crown was added later and from 1867 a letter was added under the factory mark to indicate the year

Wedgwood

Instead of symbols, the Wedgwood factory used its name, either impressed or printed. The words 'Made in England' were added from about 1910 onwards

Founded 1754 by the multi-talented Josiah Wedgwood, who conducted many chemical experiments which enabled him to bring new techniques to the factory. These included the famous Queen's Ware, Caneware, Basalt and of course Jasperware. Wedgwood was influenced by the Classical revival and his motto was 'elegant simplicity'.

Derby

Established in 1755 by William Duesbury, who later purchased both the Chelsea and Bow factories. Bone ash was introduced into the Derby works soon after the Chelsea factory was bought in

1770. Eighteenth-century Derby ware was celebrated for its brilliant groundlaying colours, particularly the blue lapis lazuli and later an underglaze cobalt blue. The factory employed some painters of note, including William Billingsley, 'Quaker' Pegg and 'Jockey' Hill. The prefix 'Crown' was used in their title after a visit by Queen Victoria in 1890.

Lowestoft

Founded 1757. Produced everyday blue and white soft paste porcelain. It is said that many of the primitive designs were painted by the local fishermen's wives! Later, souvenirs (trifles) were decorated with messages such as 'A trifle from Lowestoft', a trend which many factories followed. Chinese porcelain made for the export market was often wrongly attributed to Lowestoft. Lowestoft had no factory mark of its own, but used decorators' numbers instead; it also copied Worcester and Meissen marks.

There were, of course, many other factories worthy of mention, but as space is limited there is not room to list them all. Look in your local library for books with details of factories such as Derby, Spode, Coalport and Doulton, which make very interesting reading for the serious china painter.

Feature Factory: Royal Doulton

The Doulton factory was founded in 1815 by John Doulton, who invested £100, his life savings, in an obscure pottery in Lambeth, south London. Since then the factory, now known as Royal Doulton, has grown into one of the world's leading porcelain producers. In the eighteenth century it made stoneware jugs and flasks, and as production flourished a larger factory was built. In 1835 fifteen-year-old Henry Doulton joined the company, and his talent and enthusiasm were to be responsible for Doulton's rise to world acclaim. Under Henry's driving force the pottery produced decorative pieces, many of which won major awards at the Paris Exhibition of 1867. For the 1871 First International Exhibition to be held in London, artists and sculptors worked together to make seventy pieces which created great public interest. Queen Victoria commissioned several pieces for use at Windsor Castle, and the Royal Family became great admirers of Doulton ware.

The Derby factory used many marks, including the one above, which shows the Chelsea–Derby connection 1770–84. The factory also used imitation Meissen and Sèvres symbols 1785 to 1848

The Royal Doulton mark centres around four interlocking letter Ds as can clearly be seen here. The word 'Royal' indicates the status, bestowed on the company in 1901 by King Edward VII

In 1882 Henry and his brother James bought a major new pottery in Burslem in Staffordshire, where 'quality and prompt execution of orders' were paramount. The finest designers and sculptors were employed and given scope for great individuality, and the Burslem pottery soon achieved quality status. In 1884 the company began to make bone china, and as world demand for tableware grew a whole new potential established itself and the factory thrived.

In 1885 Henry Doulton was awarded the Albert Medal of the Society of Arts; he also received a knighthood for his services to ceramic art and science, the first potter to receive such an honour. At the Chicago Exhibition in 1893 an American critic wrote, 'Doultons have completely outstripped their rivals and are today the leaders in English pottery.' This was due in no small measure to the creativity of Charles J. Noke, who had sculpted many fine pieces for that exhibition. He was to be a leading figure in the history of the company, making figurines and flambé wares which created a stir among connoisseurs.

In 1901 King Edward VII gave the company the seal of approval with the bestowal of the Royal Warrant, and the right to use the word 'Royal' in their title. The new Royal Doulton was directed by Henry Lewis Doulton, who took over on the death of his father in 1897.

The company has received numerous awards for it's work and the factory is today busier than ever, producing tableware of quality and of course the ever popular figurines. Such is the popularity of this factory that a Royal Doulton Collectors' Society has been formed, with branches all over the world. Exhibitions and demonstrations are mounted, and an excellent illustrated newsletter is produced regularly.

Figurines

How They are Made

Since porcelain was first made it has been the perfect medium for making figurines. By the very nature of the material it is possible, because of its plasticity, to make fine models. These original figures are made by a skilled sculptor, and from them moulds are made – up to sixty for a very complex figure.

The moulds are assembled and then liquid clay (called slip) is poured into them. The moulds are very absorbent and draw out all the water from the slip. When all the water has been absorbed by the moulds, they are removed. The pieces then have to be assembled by a 'repairer', who joins the pieces with slip so that every seam is smoothed away and the joins cannot be seen.

The figurine is then placed in the kiln. During firing the pieces fuse together, making a whole figure which is then decorated – first with a glaze which has to be fired again, and then by the artist who will paint the face and the clothing with onglaze enamels. The faces on figurines need to be very delicately painted, and factories employ highly skilled painters for this purpose. I once read that some factories employ only male painters for this task, as they fear that women artists would be prone to paint an idealized version of themselves or an image of the latest film or soap star! Faces are always hand-painted (it would be almost impossible to place a transfer over a moulded face), but sometimes on cheaper figures the clothing is transfer-decorated. Different factories have their own style of decorating the garments on their figures and their products may be easily recognized in this way.

The History of Figurines

Among the best English figurine manufacturers in the past were Bow, Chelsea, Derby, Minton, Worcester and of course Doulton. Some of these venerable factories are still producing figurines today. Famous Doulton and Royal Doulton figure modellers include Charles J. Noke, who created many of the 'Prestige' figures, George Tinworth, Leslie Harradine, Peggy Davies and Eric Griffiths. The tradition began in Staffordshire, where figures were made from 1720 onwards; and between 1745 and 1793 they were made by all the major factories. However, during the nineteenth century there was a decline in standards of modelling by some factories and the popularity of figures waned until early this century.

Early English figures often depicted literary characters or actors, while later, in the nineteenth century, they showed contemporary politicians, generals, royalty and well-known personalities including murderers and prize fighters! With the increase in demand for figures in the new style, techniques developed often in a more Classical style. Later figures were to be made in categories with a theme such as fair ladies, historical characters, children and nursery rhymes.

Much of the revival in the interest in figurines is due to Charles

Royal Doulton 'Myths and Maidens': Juno and the Peacock.
Photograph: Royal Doulton Limited

Royal Doulton 'Prestige' figure: Jack Point.
Photograph: Royal Doulton Limited

J. Noke, Director of Design from 1912 to 1936 at the Royal Doulton factory, whose skill as a figure modeller was in evidence as early as 1893 where he exhibited several small sculptures at the Chicago Exhibition. He had been interested in ceramic sculpture since his childhood days, spent in his father's antique shop.

Collecting

Collectors soon caught on to the idea that older pieces were worth seeking, and today they command high prices at auction. Even new figures can be expensive, due to the labour-intensive medium of production. Some of Noke's earliest figures such as *Jack Point*, for instance, are still being made today; these 'Prestige' figures cost several hundred pounds.

As I have mentioned, part of my work is as a ceramics restorer and many figurines are brought in for repair. It gives me much pleasure to 'own' these lovely pieces just temporarily. Most of them of course I couldn't afford to buy, and there are those that I hope my customers will not pick up – however, they always do!

There is no doubt that the collecting of figurines is a very popular pastime for many thousands of people, and specially arranged shows are held each year for them.

How to Clean Figurines

First place a towel or piece of rubber foam in the bottom of the kitchen sink, and then add mild detergent and warm water. Gently wash the figures with a soft brush, taking care not to damage delicate areas such as the fingers or ears, or any other part of the figure which could easily become dislodged. Rinse in clean warm water. As figures are hollow, you may like to block the hole in the base with Blu-tak or a cork. However, some water will still seep in, so it is advisable to place the rinsed figure on a soft cloth until completely dry, which could take several hours.

If a figure is extremely dirty, with ingrained grime accumulated over a period of years, the following solution will remove it without too much effort. Fill a small bowl with warm water and add one tablespoon of Ariel detergent and a teaspoon of Calgon water softener. Leave the china to soak for about fifteen minutes. You will find that most of the ingrained dirt has been lifted off, though you may need to use a soft make-up brush for intricate areas. Discretion must be used when cleaning bisque figures (figures with a matt appearance and no glaze), as some colours and gold can be worn away with vigorous cleaning.

Displaying Figurines

This is of course a matter of personal preference. If you are lucky enough to own a beautiful old 'Prestige' figurine it will stand alone, but if like most collectors you have a selection of figures a little thought should be given to their position and lighting. In all cases they should be placed where passing traffic can do no damage, and a cabinet or corner shelf is ideal. If, like me, you want to display them on your mantelpiece, do what I do and place three small pieces of Blu-tak under each one, which will stop them being accidentally brushed off during dusting. If you have a cat your figures should be displayed in cat-free areas – as a restorer I get more pieces that have been knocked over by Pussy than damaged in any other way!

ODE TO A PORCELAIN FIGURE

Who was the potter that shaped the clay
Moulding your hands with delicate grace,
Dressed you in garments of yesterday,
And captured the calm of your lovely face?

Whose was the beauty so still and serene
That charms my heart when I glance your way?
Were you mother, or maid, or only a dream –
Ideal of woman enshrined in clay?

For man will dream, and the things he dreams
Are the shape of the world he wants to be –
But where is the one to take hold of the dream
And fashion the form for all to see.

For the dream is born of the heart's desires
In its outward reach as it strives to find
The beauty to which the soul aspires –
And he finds it all in his questing mind.

Mavis Quartermaine, Kalgoorlie, Australia

Royal Doulton 'The Gentle Arts': Painting.
Photograph: Royal Doulton Limited

Art Deco figurine with lustres

Figurine Project: Art Deco Figure

When buying your china or porcelain figure to decorate, do examine it thoroughly. Often the faces are badly modelled, and no amount of careful painting can disguise a pug nose or lopsided mouth – you will end up with an ugly-looking figurine. Don't forget to look at it from the side view, too. Check also that there isn't an area of unglazed china and fire cracks in the base and on the hands. A further fault to look out for is the section where the hands meet the dress. Often this is badly moulded, and if so you will experience trouble when you come to paint the hands. You don't want your figure to look as if she is wearing mittens! Small flaws on the gown may be overpainted with little trouble by covering them with a sprigged flower, for instance.

If you have never painted a figurine before, try painting in one colour or with lustre, like the ones illustrated. The gold and white one was done first with liquid bright gold, and then with burnishing gold on the second fire. If you use gold, be especially careful not to make mistakes with the brush. Removing gold can be difficult, and you will be left with purple smears. These can, however, be removed after firing with a gold eraser or Vanish (a solution containing hydrofluoric acid, used for removing fired colour).

The Art Deco figure is, in my opinion, one of the nicest to decorate. For this one I used two coats of mother of pearl lustre, firing between each, plus black and gold; the only splash of colour was on the red hair.

ART DECO FIGURE

Colours used:
Mother of pearl lustre, black, burnishing gold, ivory, blush pink, dark brown, yellow-red

Number of fires:
Five

Notes:
Apply the burnishing gold fairly thinly. If lustre is applied too thickly, it will fire away altogether

---

1st Fire
Paint in the black areas, then the face and hands, using ivory and blush pink, with dark brown for the eyebrows. Fire at 800°C.

2nd Fire
Add shading to these areas as necessary. Fire again at 800°C.

3rd Fire
Apply mother of pearl lustre (make sure you apply it over the black flowers on the dress). Paint the hair with yellow-red. Fire at 740°C.

4th Fire
Apply burnishing gold. Allow it to dry for several hours and then give it another coat, being careful not to lift the previous unfired gold. Fire at 740°C. Burnish gold after firing.

5th Fire
Apply another coat of mother of pearl lustre. Fire at 740°C.

Alternative colour suggestions: pale blue lustre with royal blue; black lustre with gold; clover lustre with American beauty.

Dancing Figure

The Dancing Figure was also done with lustre. This time I used dark blue on the beret and skirt, applying three coats to get an even, dark covering, and firing between each one. Over this I finally applied a coat of mother of pearl lustre to give more iridescence. The inside of the skirt was painted with red baby roses and small leaves.

A Note for Teachers
Here's a tip for dealing with the tiresome job of transporting figures to the kiln for firing. I use a pencil holder (the wooden block variety) filled with pencils, each holding a blob of Blu-tak. The figurines are then placed over each pencil and they hold quite firmly on the way to the kiln. If you intend painting a lot of figurines it is worth making a more permanent holder for them.

Did You Know
You can fire porcelain which has been secured with Blu-tak, as it will burn away in the kiln and turn to dust (don't forget to clean

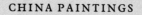

Figurines with lustres and gold decoration.
Left: Dancing Figure
Right: Note the badly moulded face on the gold figurine, giving
her a pug-nosed appearance. Try to avoid this fault

out the dust afterwards though). This is a wonderful way to paint jewellery as you can secure several blanks with Blu-tak to a tile (the unglazed side). This will enable you to paint without holding them, and they are fired as they are, on the tile.

Clarice Cliff

The best-known exponent of ceramics during the Art Deco period was surely Clarice Cliff. Her flair for colour and design was considered by many to be outrageous, and echoed the often uninhibited lifestyle of the twenties and thirties. Her colourful designs transcended the dull surroundings of the Potteries where she worked for many years, first as an apprentice and later as chief designer to two factories, with other staff painting her designs. One of eight children, Clarice was born in 1899 in Tunstall, Staffordshire into a working-class family, where scope for achievement was limited. There was nothing in her childhood to suggest that she would one day become a shining star in the Potteries' crown. Her interest in ceramics began at school where she made clay models, and during her visits to a 'pot bank' where her aunt worked and where she was allowed to play with lumps of clay.

Children started work early in those days in working-class families, and at the age of thirteen Clarice started as an apprentice in the enamelling trade, where she was paid one shilling a week as a freehand painter on pottery. As most of the men were away fighting in World War I at this time, opportunities for women were presented. Clarice readily took advantage of these, and her parents, realizing her neglected talent, paid for her to attend Tunstall School of Art.

Clarice worked hard and eventually joined the firm of A. J. Wilkinson as a lithographer. With the support of the firm's director, Colley Shorter, and that of Jack Walker, the chief designer, she developed her flair for design. Later Clarice was to lead a team of girls, all under her instruction and painting her designs. They were called 'The Bizarre Girls', after the colourful series of ware which was given this name and which reflected the Jazz Era.

Looking closely at some of this ware, it may often seem to us, as fine china painters, crudely decorated. But like it or not, it possessed a unique style and flair which at the time was very refreshing, and in its day it was startlingly original. For her designs she used bright clear colours such as Harrison's tangerine and Sèvres green often outlined with black. It is now extremely collectable, ensuring that the name of Clarice Cliff, who came from such humble beginnings, will always be synonymous with pottery of the twenties and thirties. Interestingly, though most pieces were marked 'Hand-painted by Clarice Cliff', most of these would have been decorated by the team of girls that worked under her.

Pages 42 and 43 show four of my versions of the Clarice Cliff style, using strong blocks of colour. In the early years Clarice instructed 'her girls' to apply the colour unevenly so that the brushmarks would show, indicating that the pieces were all hand-painted. However, in later years she changed her ideas and the colour was painted in a more even manner. Use these designs to decorate vases, pots and mugs.

Many museums have collections of Art Deco pieces, and there is a Clarice Cliff Collectors' Society.

Clarice Cliff Style Project: Cottage and Trees

For my Clarice Cliff style piece I've used the idealized cottage theme with fir trees that Clarice loved so much. This design is a

Stylized cottage and trees. This design looks good around the base of a vase or teapot. Keep the colours clear and bright

'Fantastical' trees

bit 'twee', but fun to do, and if you use good, strong colours it can be attractive.

I use fat oil as a medium for this style of painting. The colours should be clear and bright and painted in flat blocks. Most of the designs can be completed in two fires – one if you can get the colour on strong enough and keep it crisp and clear. But with this rather primitive style of painting I prefer to paint the bright colours in one fire and the black outlines on a second fire. If you are using bright scarlets and tangerines, remember to fire these no higher than 760°C and to use a scrupulously clean brush or your reds will fade. Apply these colours on the last fire. If painting on cylindrical-shaped pieces, do not apply the colour so thickly that it will run down on firing; it is better to take an extra fire if in doubt.

1st Fire
Block in the strong colours as evenly as you can, with no shading. Fire at 780°C (unless using reds and tangerines – see above).

2nd Fire
Outline the design in black. Fire at 770°C.

On the four designs I have suggested, I have painted the background on the orange and the green design, and allowed a little turps to be run through it to create a mottled effect. A similar technique has been used on the butterfly background, but to a lesser degree.

*Four of my own designs in the Clarice Cliff style. The colours
are clear and bright and applied in a flat, opaque wash*

A Clarice Cliff vase, shape 370, decorated in her Red Roofs design, which was produced from 1931 to 1932.
Photograph: Clarice Cliff Collectors' Club

Small plate with Clarice Cliff style cottage

Roses

Oh my love is like a red red rose
That's newly sprung in June,
Oh my love is like the melody
That's sweetly played in tune.

Robert Burns

Could there be an England without roses? Surely the rose is the flower most written about: whole books have been devoted to its beauty, its place in the garden, its importance in perfumery and medicine, and most of all its uses in decoration of all kinds, including ceramics, textiles, heraldry and flower arranging. The rose existed long before man, and fossils of rose plants millions of years old have been found in America, Europe and Asia. Evidence suggests that roses were originally native to the northern hemisphere and later taken south of the equator by man.

Many cultures have their own folklore regarding the rose, but all view it as the goddess of flowers. A Roman poet wrote that the rose 'fell from the hair of Aurora as she combed it'. Botticelli painted Venus rising from the sea in a spray of roses. Medieval legend held that in the Garden of Eden grew a white rose, which when Eve kissed it blushed and turned into a red rose. The Virgin Mary is closely associated with roses, and it is said that she appeared at Fatima in Portugal and at Lourdes in France from a circle of roses. The origin of the rosary is associated with the chaplet of beads, perfumed with roses, given to St Dominic. The Greeks grew roses in silver pots, and in Rhodes the flower grew in abundance and was often stamped on ancient coins.

Further afield, large quantities of roses were grown in the Nile Valley, and Egyptian kings and queens were buried in rose-filled tombs. In China the rose is thought to have been grown as early as 2700 BC, and in the fourth and fifth centuries AD, according to Confucius, the Imperial Library contained as many as six hundred books devoted to the flower. Rich people of the time perfumed themselves with attar of roses, whilst the common people carried dried rose petals. In Persia, Omar Khayyam mentioned it many times in his poetry, and a rose grew on his grave in Nishapur. Rose motifs were used on Persian and Turkish ceramics from the sixteenth century onwards.

In medieval monasteries, monks grew roses in their gardens and from them made many perfumes and potions. Both the rose

Roses

Sheila Southwell

Roses on a framed porcelain plaque
(Collection Mr and Mrs B. Newman)

petals and the hips were used, and these monastery gardens were havens of tranquillity. The sovereigns of England used the rose in various forms in heraldry. The stylized Tudor rose, symbolizing the combined red rose of Lancaster and white rose of York, was very much in evidence during and after the reign of Henry VII. The crown and the rose were often used together as a mark of excellence, and hostelries all over the country were named 'The Rose and Crown'.

At the Palace of Malmaison in France, the Empress Josephine had one of the most famous rose gardens of all times, and she employed many gardeners to take care of them. Her agents were sent all over the world to acquire different species, and during the Napoleonic Wars they alone were allowed to pass unmolested between England and France. Her interest in the flower stimulated the cultivation of the rose and artists were employed to record the many species. The most famous of them was Pierre-Joseph Redouté, whose best-known work, *Les Roses*, was published in three volumes after Josephine's death in 1817.

In the sentimental code of the old Language of Flowers, most species had only one meaning, but the rose commanded twenty-two meanings covering all its various colours and forms. The red rose means I love you; the yellow rose – jealousy; the cabbage rose – ambassador of love; the musk rose – capricious beauty; a white rosebud – girlhood; the dog rose – pleasure and pain; the white rose – I am worthy of you; and so on.

Roses more than any other flower symbolize romantic love. Passionate declarations of love have been written by poets, their words lavishly illustrated with garlands of roses.

Rose Project: Framed Plaque

The large rose plaque illustrated was painted on a tile which had a pale cream background when I purchased it, so when painting it I deliberately left little 'windows' of the cream colour showing through. The tile was then mounted on to a strong board covered with matching fabric, which was placed into the frame. A word of warning – when mounting these heavy tiles, you must make several holes in the fabric so that the tile is glued directly on to the board backing as well as on to the fabric. If you do not do so, the weight of the tile will pull the fabric away from the board backing and make it buckle. Also be sure to use a heavy nylon cord for hanging.

ROSE PLAQUE

Colours used:
Pale yellow, Pompadour pink, yellow-red, dark green,
leaf green, mid-brown, malachite blue

Number of fires:
Three

Notes:
Most of the work on the flowers should be done on the
first firing. Make plenty of strong highlights. Ensure the
flowers look as though they are trailing down

1st Fire

Sketch or trace your roses on to the tile and apply the background shading around the design. Paint a wash of pale yellow over the leaves. Most of the rose painting is done on this fire, using Pompadour pink shaded with yellow-red. Keep nice sharp highlights, and make the rose paler on the side where the light is coming from. Clean out the little stamens with your wipe-out tool. Fire at 800°C.

2nd Fire

Using dark green filter your background in the most shaded part of the design, tuck the colour right under the leaves and flowers. This will bring the design forward. Use some Pompadour pink in the background to echo the pink in the roses. Now, with leaf green and a little mid-brown, start shading your leaves. Do not cover the whole leaf, but allow some of the yellow from the first fire to show through. Paint the shadows under turned back leaves with this same colour. On the shadow side of the roses paint the darker areas with Pompadour pink and also the deep throat of the rose. Maintain plenty of highlights. Fire at 800°C.

3rd Fire

Add any darks to the background and now paint in the stems of the roses and leaves, using a warm brown. Don't forget to add a few thorns. Put the finishing touches to the leaves, adding one or two veins at this stage. Paint in a tiny amount of malachite blue, very pale, in the background. Fire at 800°C.

3. France

*The Eiffel Tower, Paris – the most universally
recognized symbol of everything French*

Sèvres cache-pot

Early French earthenware probably dates back to the fourteenth century and consisted of buff-coloured unglazed ware. Later, in the fifteenth century, glazed jugs were in evidence, and pieces made of brown clay with applied designs and green-glazed dishes with relief mouldings have been found. The medieval wares were the forerunners of the finer sixteenth-century pottery of Avignon and Beauvaisis, and at Nevers in the seventeenth century faience (tin-glazed earthenware, also known as maiolica) with a beautiful deep blue ground was made. Faience continued to be made at several potteries including Lille, St Cloud, Chantilly and Mennecy, but chief among them was the Vincennes-Sèvres factory. These factories, all except Lille in the Paris area, were to produce some of the finest porcelain ever made. The later Sèvres, though still of great importance, is not considered to be as exquisite as that of the earlier years.

The Limoges area of France is also of great importance, as a deposit of china clay was found at St Yrieix in the eighteenth century. A great deal of modern porcelain is made in this area, notably Haviland whose company history makes excellent reading. Quimper in Brittany is also an area of note, famous for its attractive peasant pottery which has been made for several centuries and is still in demand today.

Feature Factory: Sèvres

What we call the Sèvres factory was actually founded in the Château de Vincennes in 1738 with workmen from the Chantilly factory. Sèvres was the French national porcelain factory, and it led European ceramics fashion from 1760 until 1815. Products of the Vincennes period are of soft paste porcelain, which was used exclusively until 1768 and quite often until 1800. In 1756 the factory moved to Sèvres and was taken over by King Louis XV, who became its principal client. From 1758, in the King's dining room at Versailles, an annual sale took place at which the courtiers were expected to buy! Madame de Pompadour also had a share in the company and exercised her influence here too.

Sèvres porcelain was famous for its beautiful grounded colours: the dark *gros bleu* was used from 1749, the turquoise *bleu céleste* from 1752, the *jaune jonquille* yellow from 1753 and a pretty pea green from 1756. Later a *rose Pompadour* was used, until about 1766.

Wealthy people of this period loved the opulence of these

Sèvres was originally established at Vincennes and early marks show interlocking letter Ls. This mark shows the date letter of 1754 pieces decorated in clear bright grounds with reserved panels (panels of decoration on a plain-coloured ground) painted with flowers, birds or figures in the style of the artist Boucher. These brilliant pieces were executed without a trace of vulgarity and are still among the world's most expensive and sought after porcelain. Later decoration was richly embellished with raised enamels and pastes and painted in gold, silver and colours to resemble precious jewels – hence the name 'jewelling'. Often scenes with mythological and sentimental themes were painted, ensuring great popularity. At this time, by order of the King, no other factory was allowed to make porcelain; and even after this rule was relaxed, no factory was allowed to imitate the pieces decorated with coloured grounds.

In 1793, after the Revolution and the execution of Louis XV, the factory was declared state property and the letters 'R F' (République Française) used as a mark in place of the royal cypher. After this, much plain white porcelain was sold off to independent painters, many of them English, to be painted in their own studios (sounds familiar!). Staff numbers were reduced and production almost halved.

However, in 1800 Alexander Brongniart was appointed director and he quickly put the factory on its feet again by abandoning the expensive manufacture of soft paste. Instead he developed a new formula for hard paste and manufactured a whole new range of pigments. The factory at this period was widely patronized by Napoleon for whom some superb pieces were made, often depicting scenes of his own victories, and eminent artists such as J. B. Isabey were employed to execute these paintings. The factory created an Empire style of ceramics which was imitated by other European factories and remained popular for many years after Napoleon's death.

After 1815, decoration became increasingly fussy and quantities of plaques featuring famous oil paintings were produced. But after reorganization of the factory in 1848, many of the painters copying these Old Masters were sacked. Greater attention was now paid to the actual quality of the porcelain, and paler, softer colours were used in decoration. The *pâte-sur-pâte* technique (see p. 65) was developed by Marc Louis Solon, and the factory moved to new premises near St Cloud in 1876. New sculptors and artists were employed, and pieces with an Oriental influence made an appearance. In the first half of the twentieth century pieces in the Art Nouveau and Art Deco style were in evidence, but the factory was then, and still is, mainly engaged in making beautifully executed copies of eighteenth-century wares.

No porcelain has been as consistently well documented and marked as Sèvres since 1753, with the exception of biscuit figures for which no factory mark was applied until 1860. Many books have been devoted to this factory, and make excellent reading.

Sèvres Style Project: Ribbon Garland Vase

For the Sèvres style I have chosen a classic-shaped vase which lends itself to the French style of painting. I have used ribbon garlands with small baby roses and forget-me-nots on a salmon pink ground.

RIBBON GARLAND VASE

Colours used:
Salmon pink, royal blue, baby blue, yellow, moss green,
liquid bright gold

Number of fires:
Three

Notes:
When painting ribbon garlands, make sure that the twists
and turns look like ribbon and shade them accordingly.
Plain shapes are better suited to the Sèvres style of
painting, and if using spaced panels check your
measurements carefully before starting to paint. It also
helps when groundlaying a vase to tape protective tissue
inside to prevent powdered colour dropping into the vase,
giving you a tedious cleaning up job. ALWAYS wear a
face mask when groundlaying loose powered colour

1st Fire
Groundlay the centre part of the vase with salmon pink which has been sieved to remove any gritty particles. Fire at 820°C.

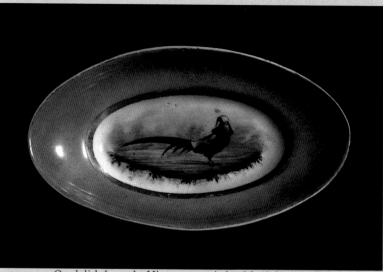

Oval dish from the Vincennes period, with pink groundlay
(Author's Collection)

Vase painted in a Sèvres style design

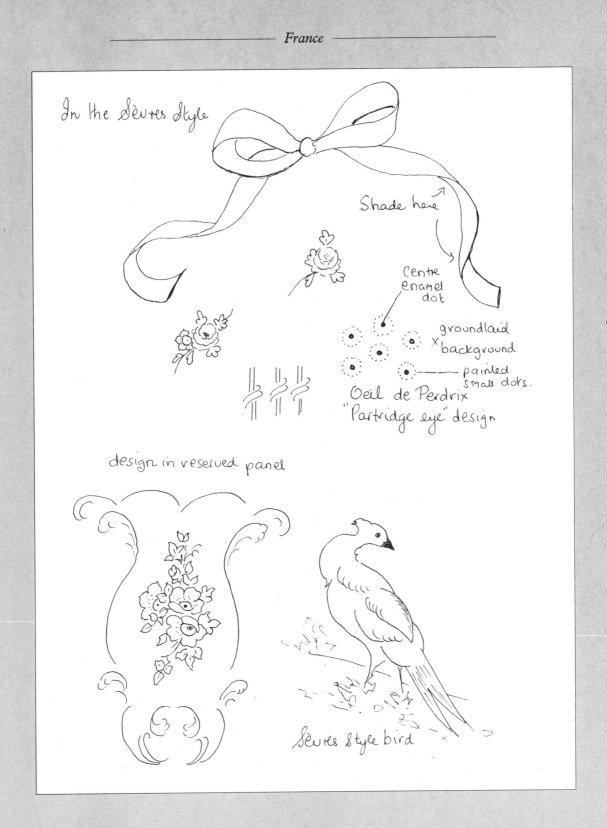

In the Sèvres Style

Shade here

Centre enamel dot

groundlaid x background

painted small dots.

Oeil de Perdrix "Partridge eye" design

design in reserved panel

Sèvres style bird

2nd Fire

Measure out the garland areas and paint the baby roses and forget-me-nots. Paint the vertical strokes with dark blue, ensuring that they are straight. If you can manage it on this fire, paint the ribbons. (You may find it easier to allow another firing for this.) Fire at 820°C.

3rd Fire

Apply the bright gold with a pen. Fire at 740°C.

Art Nouveau Plate with Poppies, Lustre and Satin Gold Metallic

At the turn of the century in Paris, a new style of art and design emerged and influenced most aspects of the decorative arts. It was called Art Nouveau and was characterized by highly stylized floral patterns, curving lines and sensuous female forms with long, flowing hair. This 'New Art' reached its height of popularity before World War I and is now once again in vogue, with the reprinting of books illustrating these designs. It is a 'fun' style of painting for the porcelain decorator, and by using lustres many

Some Art Nouveau decorations

interesting and colourful designs may be obtained. Look out for complementary porcelain shapes for this interesting art form.

ART NOUVEAU PLATE

Colours used:
E.S. yellow-red no.22, soft turquoise blue, black, liquid bright gold, mother of pearl lustre, satin gold metallic, white raised enamel

Number of fires:
Five

Notes:
ALWAYS wear a mask when groundlaying. The satin colours are particularly 'heavy' and remain in the atmosphere for several hours after using them. Keep your fingers off the warm gold and lustre on removal from the kiln. Make sure you use a reliable red – avoid the cadmium-selenium reds. Fire satin very hot, at 850°C

1st Fire
Outline the whole design lightly with pale grey, but paint the poppy stems with deep black and make them thicker than the other outlines. Fire at 800°C.

2nd Fire
Mask out the shapes around the edge of the poppies and ground-lay with satin gold. Remove the masking fluid. Fire at 850°C.

3rd Fire
Paint the poppies, their centres and the buds. Fire at 780°C.

4th Fire
Paint the leaves with liquid bright gold. Apply a little raised white enamel to the flower centres. Fire at 760°C.

5th Fire
Cover the gold leaves with mother of pearl lustre. Fire at 740°C.

Art Nouveau poppies with lustre and satin gold metallic ground

Sheila Southwell

Art Nouveau Poppies

Normandy Portrait

The idea for this portrait came partly from a photograph taken on holiday and partly from a book on the costumes of northern France. The little girl's bonnet is trimmed with ribbon and lace and embroidered with roses and leaves, while the collar is of stiff lace.

NORMANDY PORTRAIT

Colours used:
Flesh, portrait grey, blonde flesh, pale chestnut, warm flesh pink, copen grey, blue, black, rose pink, shading green, ochre

Number of fires:
Four

Notes:
Make sure that your subject matter is centrally placed on your china. Avoid any harsh lines by gently blending with a soft brush; this applies particularly on the cheeks. Draw the face on paper first. Then hold it up to a mirror, which will show if you have one eye higher than the other. NEVER sketch a portrait straight on to the china; it will rarely come out properly. If you do it on paper, then trace it on to the china with graphite paper, the features should be correctly placed. Hold the tracing in place with Sellotape whilst transferring it

In comparison with an adult's head the child's face is smaller in proportion to the rest of the head. The cheeks are full and chubby and the top lip protrudes. The eyes are also wider apart and the iris is almost fully exposed. The neck is short and fat – in fact small babies have no neck at all, as most new mums discover when trying to tie their first baby's bib! By the age of five or six the face has become larger in proportion to the head and the neck is longer. The child in the photograph appeared to be aged about five. As the child gets older the length of the face increases.

Whole books are devoted to the art of painting portraits. It is

Child in Normandy bonnet

Typical patterns to be found on the embroidered and beribboned
bonnets of northern France

The little girl from Normandy, after the first firing

The portrait completed

Box with pâte-sur-pâte *decoration on a royal blue ground*

something that I have only tried on a few occasions, but given more time I would like to devote a considerable amount of study to this art form. In my opinion this is an art form comparable to the painting of roses – so many forms and so many subjects.

1st Fire

When you have sketched the face on to the china, outline the design lightly with pale grey; this outline will be pulled into the design when painting. With warm flesh pink paint the contours of the face, shading the cheeks with a little ochre and flesh colour mixed together. Maintain highlights in the areas of light – i.e. top of cheeks, top of nose and chin. Paint in the shadow under the eyebrows. Indicate the eyelids with chestnut brown. Paint the iris with pale blue and the pupil with light black. Then wipe out a strong highlight on the pupil of the eye, and on the blue iris exactly opposite the highlight on the pupil. Indicate the nostrils with portrait grey and paint a light flush of colour on the child's lips with soft rose pink. Paint the eyebrows and hair with chestnut brown. Paint some colour on the collar – pale grey mixed with a little blue. Wipe out the ribbon tie with a clean brush. Paint the bonnet with copen grey, and wipe out the ribbon details and the lace around the face. Paint the roses on the bonnet with rose pink and green. Fire at 800°C.

2nd Fire

Shade the face with flesh colour and add a touch of pink on the cheeks, making sure the colours are well blended with a soft blending brush cleaned with either Genklene or alcohol to make it fluffy. Add more shadow under the eyebrow, keeping a small highlight where the fullest section is. Paint in the eyebrows with chestnut brown. Slightly accentuate the eyelids, but do not make them too pronounced. Add more blue to the eyes. Shade the areas around the nose with portrait grey, also the areas under the nose and above the lips. Paint the lips with rose pink and wipe out a highlight on the fullest part of the bottom lip and on the top lip. The area between the lips should also be painted darker now. Blend more brown into the hair, but leave the bonnet etc. until the next fire. Paint in the background with your chosen colour. Fire at 800°C.

3rd Fire

On this fire paint the hair and concentrate on the bonnet and the lace collar, making the patterns more pronounced. Fire at 800°C.

4th Fire

Complete any shading necessary on the face and hair. Add the shading to the bonnet bow under the chin. On this fire add the raised white enamel to the lace collar and the bonnet. Apply some detail with fine pen to the lace framing the face. Fire at 770°C.

Simple *Pâte-sur-Pâte* Box

Pâte-sur-pâte is a technique involving the use of white raised enamel over a dark groundlaid colour. This technique was first used by Marc Louis Solon, who developed it at the Sèvres factory in the mid-nineteenth century. He later worked at the Minton factory in England and his work is the finest to be seen using this technique. It was a tricky and expensive method of decorating porcelain in relief. Originally, the designs were painted on to unfired porcelain in successive layers of slip, each one being allowed to dry before the next was applied. The designs were then modelled with metal instruments which incised delicate designs in the raised patterns. Finally the pieces were glazed and fired. My method is easier, but a really good, dark groundlay must be applied to the porcelain or china first.

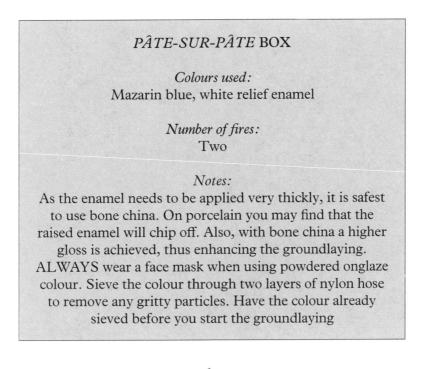

PÂTE-SUR-PÂTE BOX

Colours used:
Mazarin blue, white relief enamel

Number of fires:
Two

Notes:
As the enamel needs to be applied very thickly, it is safest to use bone china. On porcelain you may find that the raised enamel will chip off. Also, with bone china a higher gloss is achieved, thus enhancing the groundlaying. ALWAYS wear a face mask when using powdered onglaze colour. Sieve the colour through two layers of nylon hose to remove any gritty particles. Have the colour already sieved before you start the groundlaying

1st Fire
Groundlay the entire box with the dark Mazarin blue. Fire at 800°C.

2nd Fire
Prepare the white relief enamel, making it slightly thinner than you would normally have it for raised enamel work. Paint the lily and the leaves, using a No.3 sable brush. Try to get the strokes as even as possible. When the first application of enamel is dry, very gently apply another layer over it, making it stand out further in relief. If you are nervous about applying one layer over the other you may do it in separate fires. Fire at 760°C.

Pâte-sur-pâte *lilies*

4. Switzerland

A typical Swiss postcard scene,
a good subject for a china painter

Early Swiss potters were also the makers of stoves (known as Hafners), and these potters were to copy the sixteenth-century Italian maiolica techniques – pieces dating from 1542 are recorded. Winterthur was the main centre for pottery activity until the middle of the eighteenth century. Factories were also located at Lenzburg, Berne, Steckborn and Beromünster. An important Swiss pottery was the Zurich factory, which produced some of the finest porcelain made in Europe in the eighteenth century. From about 1780 hard paste porcelain was produced at Nyon. It was technically perfect, but since its designs were copied from those of the Paris factory it was considered by some to show little originality. However the Nyon porcelain, decorated with sprigs, garlands, butterflies and classic borders of great style, was much in demand and is copied by contemporary china painters. After the demise of Nyon in the mid-nineteenth century the Geneva and Langenthal factories were set up.

Feature Factory: Nyon

The Nyon factory mark, showing the symbol of fishes in underglaze blue, was used during the eighteenth century

The Zurich factory is often referred to as the finest porcelain factory in Switzerland, but Nyon must surely run a close second and its style of painting is more familiar to the hobby china painter. The Nyon factory was founded in 1780 by Ferdinand Müller, who from 1781 was in partnership with Jacob Dortu. The porcelain is of a flawless hard paste, often decorated in imitation of Paris ware: cups, coffee-pots etc. were painted with sprigs of flowers and butterflies in a stylized form. Later the factory was engaged in the production of cream-coloured earthenware and imitated Wedgwood stoneware. The factory closed in 1860. One of the most popular patterns among china painters is the Nyon blue sprigged cornflower, often in conjunction with gold single florets. This design was copied from the Paris factory where it was known as 'The Angoulême Sprig', named after the Duc d'Angoulême.

Nyon Style Project: Angoulême Sprig Tray

Pieces painted with the blue cornflower sprig have a light, airy, fresh appearance which is suitable for all types of porcelain but looks particularly pretty on classic shapes. On this square tray I have used the small cornflower sprays with gold florets in con-

A few
Nyon style sprigs

Sheila Southwell

*Cup and saucer decorated with the Angoulême Sprig, c.1781,
from the Rue de Bondy factory in Paris. The Paris designs were
copied by Nyon, and other factories, to beautiful effect.
Photograph: John Cushion*

Nyon style sweetmeat dish

junction with the garland and lattice bells, also done in burnishing gold. The tray was fired twice only: one firing for the blue, pink and green and another for the gold and enamel.

Carefully measure out your painting area and mark with pencil where the sprigs will be painted. Now use graphite paper to trace the designs on to the porcelain (when you have painted these sprigs several times you will be able to do them freehand).

ANGOULÊME SPRIG TRAY

Colours used:
Royal blue, leaf green, rose pink, burnishing gold, white raised enamel

Number of fires:
Two

Notes:
Sketch the flower sprays on to paper first and then transfer the design on to china with graphite paper. Make sure the ribbon looks like a twisted garland. If you have trouble with it, cut a 'ribbon' of paper and twist it so you can see how twists of ribbon throw shadows. Practise painting them on a tile first

---

1st Fire
Using deep royal blue and a small pointed brush paint the small cornflowers and the tiny blue florets. Paint the leaves and stems with a clear green. Now carefully paint in the ribbon garland with pink (you can take another firing and do this separately if you wish). Using a fine pen, apply small pink dots around the ribbon. Fire at 800°C.

2nd Fire
With your finest brush paint the little florets with burnishing gold. At this stage I added a tiny dot of white enamel to the flower centres. With a pen draw the lattice bells at the corners of the tray. Apply the gold scalloped edging. Fire at 740°C. Burnish the gold after firing.

Blue Gentian Plate

The lovely blue gentian is an alpine flower often associated with Switzerland. In fact, gentians grow around the world, and in a great range of colour and size – the large yellow gentian grows to over six feet but the one we are going to paint is a small blue variety. This has the typical erect bell-shaped flower with pert leaves which grow up the stem. I have used the same design for both a watercolour and a plate.

As mentioned earlier, I almost always sketch my designs on rough paper first; it is a waste of time sketching straight on to the plate, as you will rarely get it right at the first attempt. If I am painting from live flowers I make several different sketches of the flower I am studying, from various angles. I then do the same with the leaves, often dissecting the whole plant to see how it grows. Then I put the design together. If I like a design I will use it for both china painting and watercolours.

I chose this plate for its pretty shaped edge, which I have decorated with a pen over the little embossed flowers which were moulded during manufacture. I used royal blue paint with my pen oil, and the effect gives a lacy look to the edge of the plate. The small panels around the edge were done with burnishing gold on the last fire.

BLUE GENTIAN PLATE

Colours used:
Royal blue, violet blue, yellow, yellow-green, shading green, white raised enamel

Number of fires:
Three

Notes:
It is important to get the darkest shading in the deep trumpet of the flower and under the turned back petal. Do not apply the raised enamel to EVERY petal. All the penwork must be of equal fineness – no one part of it should be allowed to dominate

1st Fire

Trace the design on to your plate. Wash some yellow over the leaves and then lightly blend in some leaf green. Paint the flowers this way. The darkest value is in the deep trumpet and under the turned back petals, so paint these parts first with a small square shader using royal blue. The rest of the flower is painted with blue and violet, gently blended together using a soft blending brush.

Gentians

Sheila Southwell

Wipe out a few highlights here and there, and wipe out the little centres inside the flower centre. Fire at 800°C.

2nd Fire

Deepen the shading on the gentian in the darkest areas and wash a little blue over the rest of the flower, maintaining the highlights. Shade the leaves with shading green, allowing a little yellow to show through the lightest areas. Do the penwork around the edge of the plate and paint the flower centres with pale green. Fire at 800°C.

3rd Fire

Add just a little white relief enamel to some of the petal edges. Paint the burnishing gold on the edge panels. Fire at 760°C. Burnish the gold on completion.

Edelweiss Plate

The edelweiss is an Alpine flower with many irregular-shaped petals which radiate from a large, fluffy centre. The flowers are creamy white and therefore suited to the wipe-out technique, and this is how I formed the flowers on the plate here.

EDELWEISS PLATE

Colours used:
Black-green, leaf green, ivory yellow, mauve, sky blue, grey

Number of fires:
Three

Notes:
The mountains should be only suggested – they must not dominate the design. Practise the flowers on a tile first before you start wiping them out on the plate; they are an unusual shape, and you need to 'feel' when they are right

---

Blue gentians
(Collection Mrs N. Watkinson)

Edelweiss in a mountain scene

1st Fire

Gently suggest the mountains in the background, using mauve and grey. With black-green and leaf green paint in the area where the flowers are to be, gently shading it away from the flower area into nothing. Indicate the flowers of the edelweiss using a toothpick or wipe-out tool. Mark the centres first and then the petals. Now with a fine pointed brush wipe out the petals individually, leaving a little paint on each one for shading. Wipe out the leaves with the brush. Make the fluffy centres and add a tiny amount of ivory yellow. Fire at 800°C.

2nd Fire

Add a little more colouring to the mountains, keeping them well in the background. Paint more dark green around the flowers and leaves, also a little mauve and blue to echo the colours in the mountains and sky. Shade the flowers lightly with leaf green and paint in the centres with ivory yellow and green, maintaining plenty of highlights. Paint the leaves with leaf green. Fire at 800°C.

3rd Fire

Paint the sky with blue. Accentuate the flowers with white enamel. Fire at 760°C.

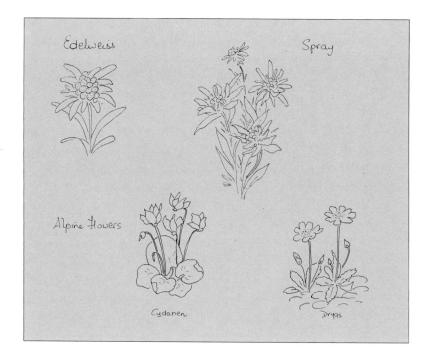

5. Denmark

The Little Mermaid, Copenhagen

The principal Danish faience factory in the eighteenth century was the Store Kongensgade, which was founded in 1722. The blue and white produced here between 1727 and 1729 was considered to be of superior quality and strongly influenced by Nuremberg. The Katstrup factory started production in about 1754 and manufactured cream-coloured wares in the English style. The porcelain factory of Louis Fournier made soft paste from 1760 to 1766 but the factory was short-lived, and the products consisted mainly of tablewares in soft enamels.

F. H. Muller's factory, founded in 1771, later became the royal factory. It made true porcelain from 1779 onwards and still exists today, known as Royal Copenhagen. The factory adopted a mark of three wavy lines, which is easily recognizable. The Bing and Grondahl factory was set up a little later, in about 1853; it is still producing beautiful porcelains at the present time.

In Denmark, as in other Scandinavian countries, china painting has long been a popular pastime with hobbyists, and painters there have produced some of the most innovative work of recent years. These Scandinavian painters are not afraid to experiment, and therefore to perfect new techniques, and this is reflected in the highly individual elegance of their porcelain decoration. The abstract designs in raised enamels, gold flaking and marbled lustres are extremely effective and suit the luminous white porcelain to perfection.

Feature Factory: Royal Copenhagen

Royal Copenhagen first used this printed factory mark, which incorporates the symbols of waves and a crown, in 1929

The making of porcelain had a number of false starts in Denmark, but in 1775 a chemist named Frantz Heinrich Müller founded a factory which was financed by a private company, although court officials were the principal shareholders. With the threat of bankruptcy in 1779, however, the factory was taken over by the Crown. At this time the trademark of three wavy lines was adopted, signifying the three ancient gateways from the Kattegat to the Baltic Sea: the Sound between Den and Sweden, the Great Belt between Zealand and Fyn, and the Little Belt between Fyn and Jutland. The crown was added to the mark in 1889.

One of the most famous works of art in the history of porcelain is the 'Flora Danica' table service, decorated by a ceramic artist named J. C. Bayer from Nuremberg. The then director, Holmskiold, insisted that the designs followed faithfully the illustrations in J. C. Oeder's book on Danish plants, *Flora Danica*, and

Flora Danica dish with lid.
Photograph: Royal Copenhagen

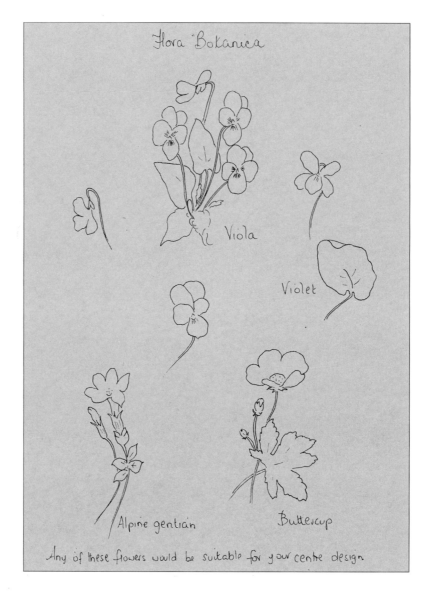

Flora Botanica

Viola

Violet

Alpine gentian

Buttercup

Any of these flowers would be suitable for your centre design

that the name of the plant be recorded on the reverse of each piece. Originally intended for Catherine the Great of Russia, the service took twelve years to complete. Before it was finished, in 1802, Catherine had died. It now belongs to the Danish Royal Family and is exhibited in Rosenborg Castle in Copenhagen.

In 1801, during the Napoleonic wars, the English attacked the Danish Fleet and in 1807 bombarded Copenhagen. This ended the shipping trade, with devastating effect on the Danish nation.

The factory's fortunes remained at a low ebb for many years. By 1867 a merchant named Falck had purchased the whole plant and the right to retain the royal name. The factory's future started to look up again in 1884, when Philip Schou bought it and spent his own money modernizing it and relocating it to Smallegade, its present location. Arnold Krog was then appointed art director and started underglaze decoration. His first piece was purchased by the Duke of Sutherland, who was yachting in the Sound, and when news of this spread, the company was once more secure – the Royal Copenhagen factory was again in business.

By 1900 shops had been opened in London, Paris and New York. Progress was slowed down for a while during World War 2 when in 1943 the plant was bombed, and imports of the necessary raw materials – kaolin from England and feldspar from Sweden – were curtailed. After the war full production was resumed, and today the factory enjoys popularity once more as a producer of fine porcelain.

Flora 'Botanica' Project: Viola Plate

VIOLA PLATE *(See p. 84)*

Colours used:
Pansy purple, Albert yellow, chartreuse, shading green, yellow-brown, dark brown, red, white raised enamel

Number of fires:
Two

Notes:
Choose a plate with a pretty moulded border (mine already had the double gold bands on it when I bought it). Your design must be botanically correct, so consult a good reference book. Do not forget to write the Latin name of the plant on the reverse side of the plate

1st Fire

Trace the design on to the china, making sure it is centrally placed. Paint the violas, using pansy purple for the two top petals and Albert yellow for the remaining four petals. The colours must be kept clear and bright and not muddied at all. Paint the leaves and stems with chartreuse. Paint the fibrous root with yellow-brown and shade it with dark brown. With shading green, and using your finger, pad a little colour all around the plate and then CAREFULLY paint the small green marks at regular intervals over the wet colour. Fire at 800°C.

2nd Fire

Apply more colour on the flowers where needed, also on the leaves and the root of the viola. With a fine brush paint the little viola buds and leaves at regular intervals around the edge of the plate. Use a fine pen to apply the dots between the buds. Place a small red dot in the centre of the violas and a little white raised enamel at each side of the centre. With a pen, apply the tiny whiskers on the flowers. Fire at 800°C.

Special Effects

Because of the random style of pattern on the illustrated pieces I am not going to explain how each was done, as most of the designs 'just happened'. What I am going to do is explain some of the various techniques used in the application of the materials necessary for this type of work.

I have found the plainer-shaped porcelain more effective with abstract designs. Some of the flat pillow vases are excellent for this work, and are easy to hold whilst working. It is better to work on one side of the vase at a time. No matter how simple the designs are meant to be, you must have a plan of action in mind before you start; it is a good idea to rough out one or two possibilities in advance.

The lustres, by their very nature, are unpredictable, but if you do not like the effect when fired you have the consolation that they may be removed with a solvent either 'Vanish' or 'Whink', leaving the porcelain quite white again. Do not allow the stripper to remain for too long on the porcelain, however, or you could remove the glaze (although this can also be effective when painted over with gold). Any fired lustre will be easily removed after the stripper has been left for only a minute or two; any small amounts of lustre which remain can be lifted with a gold eraser. Wash the piece thoroughly after removing the lustre.

If possible wear gloves when using the stripper, as it may contain hydrofluoric acid which will burn the skin. If the stripper gets on your skin, wash immediately with lots of cold water. I always take the extra precaution of wearing protective goggles.

All the following techniques are better used on porcelain. On bone china the various compounds are sometimes impossible to remove.

Gold Flaking

This is a method of removing the glaze from pieces, which may then be painted with bright gold or silver. After firing, they have a lovely crackled effect. The flaking powder is mixed with either water or copaiba oil (check supplier's instructions).

Paint the mixed compound on to the porcelain or apply it with a palette knife, putting plenty on, and fire at 850°C. After firing, chip off all the flaking mixture and it will remove the glaze from the porcelain. This is most safely done with the piece inside a polythene bag, which can then be thrown away. Cover the entire flaked area with liquid bright gold and fire at 740°C.

Another method of removing the glaze is with the use of glass beads. There are several sizes of bead for different effects. Apply a thick layer of copaiba oil and then sprinkle the beads on to it. After firing at 850°C remove the beads by chipping off (again inside a polythene bag). Then cover the area with gold, platinum or lustres, and fire at 750°C.

Marbling Lustre

Clean the porcelain first to remove all dirt and grease. Apply the lustre with a flat nylon brush and, whilst still wet, drop in small amounts of halo lustre and allow it to run. Turn the porcelain this way and that so that the lustres run together. You will not be able to control this completely, but seeing what happens is half the fun. You may drop in another coloured lustre at this stage and allow it to run into the others. This is what I did on the vase in the illustration.

Alternatively, you can paint a coat of lavender oil on the piece and whilst it is still wet drop in various lustres or gold and see what happens! Don't be afraid to experiment – you will be amazed at some of the results after firing. There are various types of medium made to produce special effects, which can be used in conjunction with lustres. They all perform differently so follow carefully the manufacturers' instructions and have fun.

A viola design

This vase is in flaked gold and marbled halo lustre. Three fires

*Seven small pieces decorated in various techniques, including
I Relief with gold, lustres and satin metallics*

*The orchid dish is in a satin metallic antique pale gold, the
flower painted with black overglaze. Two fires*

I Relief

This comes in powdered form and is mixed very thickly with copaiba oil. Then it is diluted with turps until it is stringy, rather like a normal raised enamel. Apply it with either a pointed brush or a palette knife, and make sure you put it on quite thickly. Fire at 850°C, and afterwards cover it entirely with liquid bright gold for beautiful effects. You can also use platinum, which is lovely.

Satin Metallic Colours

This is a relatively new technique and is particularly effective around borders when used as a ground. Groundlaying with these colours is much easier than with normal onglaze enamels, as the powder is very heavy and has good covering properties. It needs to be fired very high, at about 860°C, or it will not be permanent. It can be painted over with onglaze colours or used as a basis for penwork. ALWAYS wear a mask when using the satin metallic colours. Use normal copaiba oil as a basis for the groundlaying; it is not necessary to use special groundlaying oil here, but you must pad it thoroughly with silk (as with ordinary groundlaying) before applying the loose powder.

6. Thailand

*The inscrutable mystery
of an oriental deity*

Geographically and historically, factors peculiar to Thailand make it a meeting place for a whole range of art forms. The country's rich and creative history is noted particularly for its original ceramic industry. There have been several important schools of art in the country, but since the end of the eighteenth century no real unity, though there are seven main periods of importance. Despite this diversity, certain tendencies can be observed. Resulting partly from local circumstances (such as the easy availability of materials), partly from the stability of certain traditions (such as ceramics and modelling), and partly from the predominance of Buddhism, these factors are often the only real links that exist between the artistic schools that developed between the thirteenth and twentieth centuries.

In the thirteenth century there came into being the schools of thought from which the indigenous art of Thailand was to emerge. The Sukhotai School (thirteenth to fifteenth centuries) gave rise to a school of art which was extremely prolific and original in all forms of artistic activity. Its influence over the Indo-Chinese peninsula was to have a lasting effect, particularly on architecture and ceramics, which benefited from the teaching of Chinese potters. The Lan Na School (thirteenth to twentieth centuries) was partly concurrent with the Sukhotai School, from which its ceramics were influenced. The first kilns in the Chiang Mai region employed craftsmen who had moved from Sukhotai. The Ayuthia School (fourteenth to eighteenth centuries), founded in 1350, brought about a unity in artistic trends, and Bencharong ware appeared at the end of this period. The Bangkok School, active ever since the eighteenth century, followed, and has enabled us to appreciate the development of art and design in Thailand.

Bencharong Ware

One of the most exquisite porcelains in Thailand is the unique Bencharong ware. The word 'Bencharong' is derived from two Sanskrit words, *panch* meaning five and *rang* meaning colouring. Bencharong originated in China, where five-coloured enamelled ware was popular in the sixteenth century and where it was produced until 1911. The colours used in Bencharong, however, can range from three to eight. They are all applied over the glaze and one firing is sufficient for most wares, no matter how many colours are used. This is because the gold outlines are painted with

*Early nineteenth-century Bencharong jar: gold, floral and leaf
design on red enamel background*

normal oil-based gold, and the colours used are water-based onglazes; since oil and water do not mix, the designs usually fire together without any problems.

Bencharong patterns are mainly Thai, although some do show Chinese influence. In Thai designs, all the spaces between the patterns are filled in with colour and the designs are repetitive and symmetrical, often based on stylized natural forms. Many Buddhist symbols also influence the artists.

Originally, Bencharong ware was imported to the West solely for kings and wealthy people and was of exquisite quality, but later lesser-quality wares were imported for people of more modest means. The porcelain shapes are mostly utilitarian – tableware, bowls, covered boxes, water pots and so on.

A recent renewed interest in Thai arts and crafts has led to a revival of Bencharong ware. The patterns are first outlined with gold, which is allowed to dry completely before the colours and backgrounds are painted.

Bencharong Project

For this project choose a shape which reflects Oriental influence – you are more likely to find it in porcelain than in bone china. Measure carefully the spaces around the piece; otherwise when you come to join up the design at the end you will have an odd space left.

Using liquid bright gold, carefully outline the design freehand, making sure all the outlines are the same thickness. Allow the gold to dry thoroughly. Then, using water-based colours, carefully fill in the outlined designs with your chosen five colours, trying to avoid painting too much over the gold – although this may be difficult. If you have painted too much over the gold outlines, use your brush, cleaned in WATER, to tease the colour gently off the gold. Fire at about 780°C; the gold lines should fire satisfactorily at this temperature. If you are in any doubt, fire the gold first at your normal firing temperature and then fill in the colours on the second fire. Have fun.

Orchid Plaque

Orchids really are a pleasure to paint. They come in a huge range of species and colours, and thrive in the warm, humid atmosphere

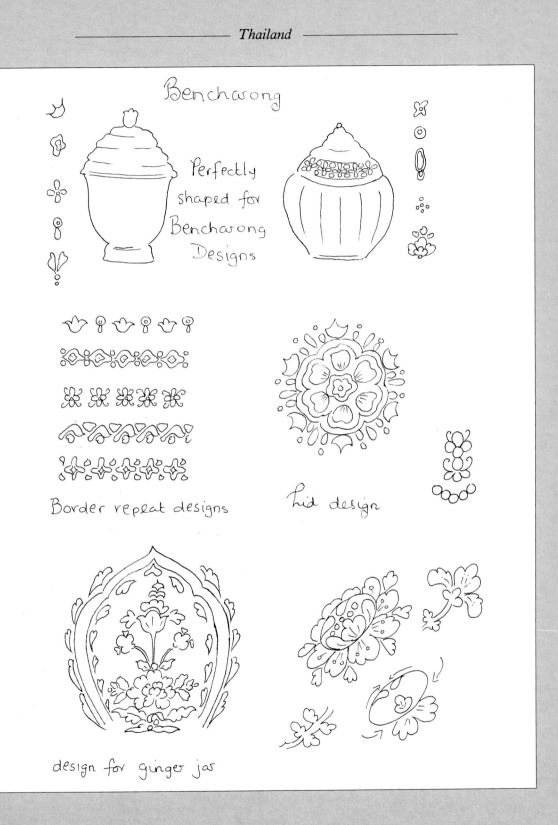

Bencharong

Perfectly shaped for Bencharong Designs

Border repeat designs

Lid design

design for ginger jar

Simple Bencharong

Pot with Bencharong design in gold, prior to colouring with enamels.
Painted by Somlak Balankura, Bangkok

Orchids on a framed porcelain plaque
(Collection S. Wakefield)

Thai orchid

An outline for the orchid plaque. Note the strap-like leaves

of Malaysia and Thailand where they grow almost like weeds – whilst we, in cooler climes, have trouble with them even in our conservatories. I have visited several orchid specialists, and when I view the flowers *en masse* I do not find them as attractive as when I look at just one flower in isolation. It is only then, in my opinion, that their true exotic beauty may be appreciated. But despite the great variation in colour and shape of the flowers, the leaves are usually strap-like and uninteresting, although they often bend and twist in an attractive way.

The tile I have painted has been mounted on matching fabric and framed in an antique copper moulding. There are several things to remember when mounting tiles. First consideration is the weight, as some of the tiles can be quite heavy. Always hang them on a good strong wire and make sure it has been properly tied at the back – these tiles can do untold damage if they fall off the wall on to a polished table! Secondly, the fabric must be fully stretched over the backing board – I usually pull mine together at the back with strong sewing twine – otherwise it will later sag and the whole thing will need to be remounted, which is tiresome.

Next, MOST IMPORTANT, you must cut a hole in the fabric so that, when you glue the tile to it, the tile itself is glued to the backing board. If you do not do this the tile will pull the fabric away from the backing and make unsightly bulges. I made three holes in this one to make sure it would hold sufficiently well. Do not cut the holes too close to the edge of the tile, otherwise when you pull and stretch the fabric you will see the holes and you will have to cut another piece.

ORCHID PLAQUE

Colours used:
Salmon pink, plum purple, chartreuse, yellow-red,
lavender blue, lime green, grey, yellow, shading green,
American beauty

Number of fires:
Three

Notes:
When firing large tiles lay them flat on the kiln shelf and
fire slowly to avoid breakages. Tiles do not have a very
thick layer of glaze, so do not expect your piece to have a
very glossy finish

1st Fire
Sketch the design on to the tile and lay a wash of lavender blue, ivory and American beauty around the main design. Then paint salmon pink over the orchids and apply a wash of chartreuse over the leaves. Wipe out a few highlights. The smaller orchids are lime green and plum purple colour. Fire at 800°C.

2nd Fire
Deepen the background colour and paint in some shadow leaves, using lavender blue mixed with a little grey. Add shading to the orchids, using salmon pink with a little yellow-red in the shadows under the petals. Remember to maintain plenty of highlights. Paint in the shading on the little orchids and on the leaves, using shading green. Fire at 800°C.

3rd Fire
Using American beauty and a fine brush, paint in the 'spots' on the petals and then pull out one or two highlights with a wipe-out tool or toothpick. Paint the yellow centres in the orchids. Deepen any background colour. Fire at 800°C.

Temple Dancer

Generally speaking I do not really enjoy painting figures, but this was a joy to decorate. Having seen the temple dancers in Bangkok with their delicate grace of movement, I couldn't get started on this one quickly enough. The main problem was how to decorate it and what colours to use, and I thought of many combinations before I finally decided on jade greens and bright orange combined with lustres.

TEMPLE DANCER

Colours used:
Jade, malachite blue, ivory, pink, ochre, brilliant orange, copper lustre, gold, mother of pearl

Number of fires:
Seven

Notes:
If you are very careful it is possible to apply the white raised enamel over the wet colour, providing you can put it on cleanly in one stroke. If in doubt, it is best to take another firing. Refer also to earlier section on figurines (p. 28)

1st Fire
Tint the flesh with a little ochre mixed with ivory and palest pink. Fire at 800°C.

2nd Fire
Using your finest brush, paint the features on the face. Paint the turban and collar with jade green. As I was holding the figure by the legs, I was also able to paint the bracelets using malachite blue. Fire at 800°C.

Thai temple dancer decorated with copper lustre and gold

3rd Fire

Holding the head of the figure, paint the top of the tunic back and front. Fire at 800°C.

4th Fire

Deepen any colours on the turban and tunic. Holding the legs of the figure, complete any facial details. Fire at 800°C.

5th Fire

Very carefully apply dots of white raised enamel on to the bracelets, collar and turban. Holding the middle of the figurine, apply a smooth coat of copper lustre to the trousers. Make sure you clean off any fingermarks first. Fire at 740°C.

6th Fire

Apply any gold you wish to the turban and collar and give the trousers another application of copper lustre. Fire at 740°C.

7th Fire

Apply bright orange (it's a cadmium colour, so use a scrupulously clean brush) quite thickly in smooth strokes. Give the trousers a coat of mother of pearl lustre. Fire at 740°C.

Lustre Butterfly Plate

Whilst in Bangkok I saw some of the most brilliant butterflies fluttering along the banks of the klongs (canals). When trying to decide on my projects for Thailand I remembered these lovely butterflies and decided to incorporate them in a lustre design for you – somehow the brilliance of the butterflies and the iridescence of the lustres seem made for each other.

When working with lustres I prefer to use English bone china, as it seems to give a superior glow to the lustre due to its soft glaze. Choose your china carefully, as any imperfections will mar the lustred finish. Clean the china with a good solvent. I always use Genklene, but if you cannot obtain it use surgical spirit, which also evaporates quickly. American china painters can use denatured alcohol, which produces a really squeaky-clean surface.

You can let your imagination run riot when choosing the colours for your butterflies. They will not necessarily have to be specific types, but rather figments (or should I say pigments) of your imagination! I have designed one large central reserved panel, with six smaller ones of differing sizes. The lustre was dark blue with a final application of mother of pearl, and I applied the lustre in several layers, firing between each, to obtain the lovely dark blue shade.

LUSTRE BUTTERFLY PLATE

Colours used: ·
Dark blue lustre, white relief enamel, grey, bright gold, many different colours for the butterflies

Number of fires:
Ten

Notes:
When using lustres make sure that the china is scrupulously clean. Penwork should be very fine and all the same depth of colour. Do not have the butterflies all the same shape and facing the same way

---

1st Fire
Decide where your butterflies are going to be, and then using pale grey mark out your reserved panels very lightly. Fire at 780°C.

2nd Fire
Carefully sketch or trace on the butterflies, and outline them finely with pen using a good-quality black onglaze colour. Fire at 780°C. If you are careful, you can do this on the first firing.

3rd Fire
Paint the butterflies and grasses in your chosen colours. Fire at 780°C.

4th Fire
Accentuate any colours on the butterflies and complete the grasses. Fire at 780°C.

5th Fire
Mask out the reserved panels completely and allow them to dry. Paint the entire plate with blue lustre, using a soft nylon brush

Butterflies

A few shapes to use for your own designs

Butterflies and lustre plate

with no loose hairs. Remove the masking fluid. Fire at 740°C. When removing the plate from the kiln after firing, keep your fingers off the lustre or you could permanently mark it.

6th to 8th Fires

Repeat the coats of lustre until the colour is dark and smoothly opaque. If it is still patchy give it as many more coats of lustre as are necessary.

9th Fire

Cover the entire blue lustre with a smooth application of mother of pearl lustre. Fire at 740°C.

10th Fire

Using white enamel, apply scrolls and dots around the reserved panels and on to the butterflies' wings where it is most effective. With a fine pen and liquid bright gold draw a few small butterflies over the blue background – but don't overdo it. Fire at 740°C.

I had a slight disaster with this plate. I originally intended to use raised paste and burnishing gold on the scrolls, dots and so on, but for some reason the gold would not burnish after firing (yes – I did use the correct paste and gold). Not wanting to fire the plate too many more times I decided to try white enamel over the paste and it worked quite well – but if you look closely you can still see the paste underneath. However it is not unattractive. There is almost always a way out of a dilemma. Mistakes – we all make 'em. But it's bad luck when they happen on the tenth fire!

7. China

Blossom, framing a Chinese pagoda

China is where it all began – the birthplace of porcelain. Pottery was made long before porcelain, as the right kind of clay was found in countries all over the world. Earthenware does not require as high a firing as porcelain, and in hot countries the pots were just left out in the sun to dry.

Chinese potters discovered the use of china clay as early as AD 210 and later, in 850, the second essential ingredient – china stone. They found that when these two materials were mixed together and fired at a high temperature they fused into a translucent mass – what we know as hard paste porcelain (see p. 24). The glaze for hard paste porcelain was also composed of china stone and was fired at the same temperature as the body. This gave a tight, smooth glaze which rarely crazed.

Later, during the Sung Dynasty (960–1279), the finest wares were decorated with incised patterns. From the mid-fourteenth century cobalt oxide was used for decoration. It was painted immediately before glazing, enabling the piece to be completed in one firing. From the end of the fourteenth century Chinese potters decorated their porcelain with enamel colours made from coloured glass, and during the seventeenth century Chinese porcelain was in great demand by European royalty and the aristocracy.

Apparently, most books on the subject in the nineteenth century were published in France, and this is the reason we use so many French phrases when referring to Chinese porcelain. *Famille verte*, *famille rose*, *famille noire* and so on refer to the colours dominant in decoration, and many of the colours used by china painters today still bear these names: celeste blue, rose Pompadour, Jaune jonquille (yellow).

The first porcelain arrived in Europe by chance, as a by-product of the tea trade. Tea is very light, and something was needed to provide ballast on the long sea voyage from the Far East. Tiny, delicate teabowls and other wares, now valuable collectors' items, were pushed down between the bundles of tea.

The Europeans liked what they saw, and soon it became the 'in' thing to own Chinese porcelain. Armorial dinner services were especially popular. An aristocratic family would send full details and a drawing of its coat of arms to China, and perhaps two years later the service would arrive. Some of the interpretations of European coats of arms were distinctly odd and amusing: lions often ended up looking like rabbits, and quite often the Chinese potters (who of course spoke no language other than their own) included the client's verbal instructions in the actual decoration!

Nevertheless such pieces gave the owner tremendous social

standing, and at that time porcelain was priced on a par with silver. It created a vogue for all things Chinese.

Chinoiserie is a term applied to articles decorated in a Western imitation of Chinese art – not always accurately, and rendered with some deference to the European techniques fashionable at the time. As early as the fourteenth century, Chinese silks were imitated in Italy, which had had contact with China through Marco Polo's expeditions, and in the late sixteenth century Chinese-style blue and white porcelain was made at the Medici porcelain factory. However the term Chinoiserie is usually reserved for objects made in the seventeenth and eighteenth centuries, notably ceramics, embroideries and furniture. Often whole rooms were devoted to this style of decoration, with spectacular results. One of the richest and most opulent Chinoiserie interiors was created at the Royal Pavilion in Brighton between 1802 and 1821 by the English Prince Regent. Architecture too followed the Chinoiserie trend, and many of the parks around palaces and country houses were embellished with a folly in the shape of a pagoda or a bridge like the one so familiar from blue and white Willow Pattern.

Ming Dynasty

Ming is the name given to the dynasty which ruled China from 1368 to 1644 and which succeeded the Mongol Yuan Dynasty. The word 'Ming' means brilliant, and so the new dynasty proved to be, both artistically and politically. When written, the Chinese language is pictographic, and the words or characters are simplified pictures of the object represented. The word 'brilliant' is depicted by the combination of the characters used for the sun and the moon – symbolizing the brightest source of light in the heavens.

By the early Ming Dynasty porcelain was an already perfected art form and the painting, in underglaze blue and red, was of the finest quality. Overglaze painting had also developed at that time, and Chinese painters were using a palette of clear, bright enamels, often combining incised or carved designs into the body of the porcelain. Sometimes these designs were concealed under the incisions, only to be revealed when held against the light.

The dragon was very much in evidence during the Ming period and has been established as a decorative symbol in all forms of art.

大明宣
德年製

Marks of the Ming dynasty refer to the reigns of various emperors. The above mark indicates the Hsuan-te period 1426 to 1435

It is especially associated with porcelain. According to one classical Chinese text 'the valley echoed with the mings of a thousand dragons'. In this context 'ming' refers to the sound that dragons make!

Ming Style Project: Dragon Plate

The subjects of Chinese painting include flowers, birds, fruit, vegetables, fish, animals – particularly dragons. Generally the dragon was considered to be a benevolent creature, a bringer of rain and emblem of the Emperor. However, each religious sect interpreted the dragon in its own particular way. The dragon represents male fertility and as such is associated with water; he may be seen rising from the waves, for instance, or writhing between misty clouds. Dragons are often painted in conjunction with other decorative symbols and the whole design may contain puns, but due to the complexity of the Chinese language this can lead to all sorts of misinterpretation!

DRAGON PLATE

Colours used:
Deep carmine blue, scarlet red, lavender blue, malachite blue, black, yellow-brown, bright yellow, yellow-red, grey, I relief, liquid bright gold, platinum

Number of fires:
Seven (one too many – this plate broke on the last fire!)

Notes:
This design is more suited to a large, plain shape, preferably oval – the dragon would be cramped on a round plate. The brighter colours look more impressive but you could also do it in blue and white and gold. Trace the design on to the plate first

---

1st Fire
Groundlay the border of the plate. Fire at 850°C (don't forget to wear face mask).

2nd Fire

With black and a fine pen, carefully draw the dragon on to the plate after transferring your original design with graphite paper. Pen lines must all be the same thickness. Using black, paint the claws, wiping out a strong highlight on each one. Paint the wings and the strong outline around the body. Fire at 800°C.

3rd Fire

Paint a wash of colour over the sky and foreground, using lavender blue, bright yellow and yellow-red. Paint the mountains with the same colours but much paler. Fire at 800°C.

4th Fire

Paint a light application of malachite blue over the dragon, making it darker in the shadow areas. Paint the belly of the dragon with grey. Apply more black to the claws, wings etc. Mix I relief with copaiba until very thick, then dilute with turps and apply to the border and mountain tops. Fire at 850°C.

5th Fire

Using the same palette as before, add more colour to the sky, foreground and mountains, and anywhere else that it is needed. Fire at 800°C.

6th Fire

Paint the tongue of the dragon bright scarlet, using a scrupulously clean brush as this is a cadmium colour and will fire away if any trace of another colour contaminates it. Lay this colour on thicker than you would normally. Paint the scales on the dragon's back using platinum, and paint the tail in grey. Fire at 740°C – no hotter, or you will lose the red.

7th Fire

Paint the red again, as it has probably faded a little on the last fire. Apply more platinum to the scales. With a pen and malachite blue draw the scale marks on the tail and body. With liquid bright gold carefully cover the I relief on the mountains and the border. Fire at 740°C.

Blue and white porcelain dish painted in underglaze blue with
three bunches of grapes. Ming Dynasty, early fifteenth century.
Diameter 37.8 cm (15 in)
Photograph: Eskenazi Ltd, London

Chinese dragon

*Tracing every line on this dragon is a tedious job – why not use
the basic outline and let your imagination do the rest?*

Dragon plate with groundlay and raised cracked gold

Bamboo Vase

With crane and lute aboard, I am homeward bound across the lake,
White clouds and leaves are flying together
My home lies in the very depths of the mountains,
Among the bamboos, the sound of reading a tiny couch and
  a humble gate.

Shen Chou (1427 – 1509)

The painting of bamboo has always held an honoured place in the decorative arts of ancient China. It found special favour in the Yuan Dynasty and was a natural subject of painters who lived their secluded lives far from the Mongol court. The bamboo symbolizes a true gentleman, strong yet pliant, maintaining integrity no matter how low the winds of circumstance may bend him. The lithe grace of this plant was perfect for Chinese brushwork and brought the painter closest to the fine art of calligraphy. The form of the Bamboo must be clearly shown, and it therefore lends itself to monochrome painting. A good bamboo painting was considered to be a virtuoso performance of the highest order.

Bamboo

BAMBOO VASE

Colours used:
Shading green, yellow-brown, carmine blue, scarlet, liquid
bright gold, burnishing gold

Number of fires:
Three

Notes:
My design was painted on porcelain, and vases seem to be
a perfect choice for the bamboo plant. The gold was fired
twice, the first firing for the liquid bright gold and the
second for the burnishing gold

1st Fire
The bamboo was painted freehand, using shading green for the
leaves and yellow-brown for the stems. A pointed No. 3 brush is
ideal for these leaves. Paint the stems first and then the leaves
overlapping them. Paint the blue on the butterflies. Fire at 800°C.

2nd Fire
Paint the scarlet part of the butterflies using a clean brush. Apply
liquid bright gold with smooth strokes. Fire at 740°C.

3rd Fire
Apply more red if it has faded on the last fire. Apply burnishing
gold over the previously fired gold. Lightly outline the leaves and
stems with a pen, using green. Fire at 740°C. Burnish the gold
after firing.

Chrysanthemum Plate

The chrysanthemum must surely be one of the most popular
flowers featured in Oriental decoration, and certainly one of the
most popular flower subjects for the china painter. There are so
many different varieties and colours to choose from – second only
to the rose – that one could paint 'mums' indefinitely. I have
chosen for the main project the naturalistic style of design, the

Vase with bamboo design and burnished gold
(Collection Mr and Mrs P. Wakefield)

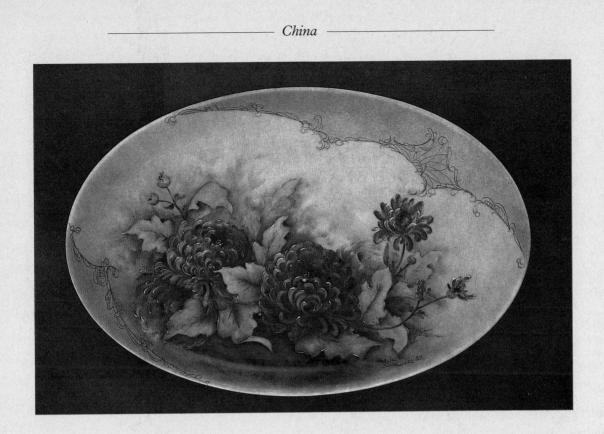

*Large plate with chrysanthemums and yellow gold satin
metallic groundlay*

flowers being wiped out of the wet background. For added interest and for something a little bit different I have used satin metallic for the edge of the plate.

CHRYSANTHEMUM PLATE

Colours used:
Satin light gold, yellow-red, yellow-brown, American beauty, Albert yellow, chartreuse, shading green, black-green, white raised enamel

Number of fires:
Five

Notes:
An oval shape is best for this large design. Complete the metallic border first. The satin colour will not be permanent unless fired very hot at 850–870°C

1st Fire

Note where the satin metallic colour is to be applied and mark out the shape with masking fluid, making the masked area about $\frac{1}{2}$ in (12mm) wide. Cover the area to be metallic-painted with copaiba oil, and then with a small ball of cotton wool covered with two layers of silk pad the oil until there is only a very smooth, light covering left on the porcelain. WEAR A FACE MASK and, with a ball of cotton wool or a large mop brush, apply the loose satin metallic colour over the oiled area, making sure that the colour is evenly spread. Using a large, soft, fluffy brush, remove all the loose colour. If the metallic colour looks uneven or if the oil is seeping through, you must remove it all and start again. When the satin colour is perfectly applied fire at 850°C.

2nd Fire

Apply American beauty and black-green to the area where the flowers are to be painted. Use plenty of colour. Use a No.3 pointed sable brush which has been cleaned in turps to wipe out the petals of the 'mums', pulling each one towards you. Wipe out the leaves, and then paint a light wash of chartreuse over them. Fire at 800°C.

The background in areas marked × should be very dark. Here
is a basic outline for your chrysanthemums. Rather than
sketching in each petal – there are dozens of them – 'feel' the
shape of the flower as you paint the petals, using one stroke only
and pulling the base of each towards a central point

Overlap each stroke towards a central point

central point

Chrysanthemums

3rd Fire

Deepen the background colour with American beauty and black-green. Filter some of the Albert yellow and yellow-red over the rest of the plate. Make the leaves more interesting with yellow-brown and shading green, and indicate one or two leaf veins. With American beauty and yellow-red wash some colour over the darkest part of the flowers, blending the colours with a soft brush. Make the centres very dark. Wipe out some strong highlights on the lightest part of the flower, keeping part of the flower in shadow. Add the stems and buds. Fire at 800°C.

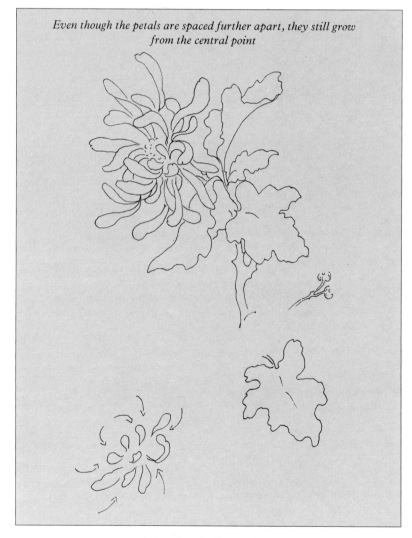

Even though the petals are spaced further apart, they still grow from the central point

Oriental-style chrysanthemum

Keep the border design simple

4th Fire
Add any more shading necessary, and paint in one or two background leaves with yellow-brown and green mixed on the brush. Filter some shadow strokes into the background with American beauty. Leave a small area of Albert yellow in the background to indicate the warmth of the sun. Adjust any highlights and petal shading. Fire at 800°C.

5th Fire
Accentuate some of the petals with white raised enamel. Then take a fine pen and use American beauty to sketch the fine scroll-work over the metallic colour. Fire at 760°C.

Blue and White Oriental Chrysanthemum Plate

Carrying on the Oriental theme I have included a simple design in blue and white. It would be equally effective in green, maroon or red.

BLUE AND WHITE ORIENTAL CHRYSANTHEMUM PLATE

Colour used:
Carmine blue

Number of fires:
One

Notes:
The flower is a 'shaggy' shape but the petals all still radiate from one central point. Each petal should be formed using one stroke only, with several overlapping

---

1st Fire
Carefully sketch the design on to the plate and then paint with carmine blue. Paint the flower and leaves first and add a border. Practise painting a border freehand on a tile first. Fire at 800°C.

8. Australia

A selection of aboriginal designs

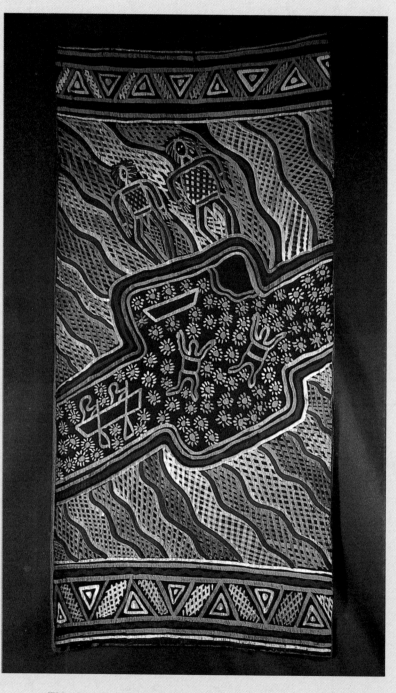

This aboriginal bark painting symbolizes figures travelling in
time through the Milky Way
(Author's Collection)

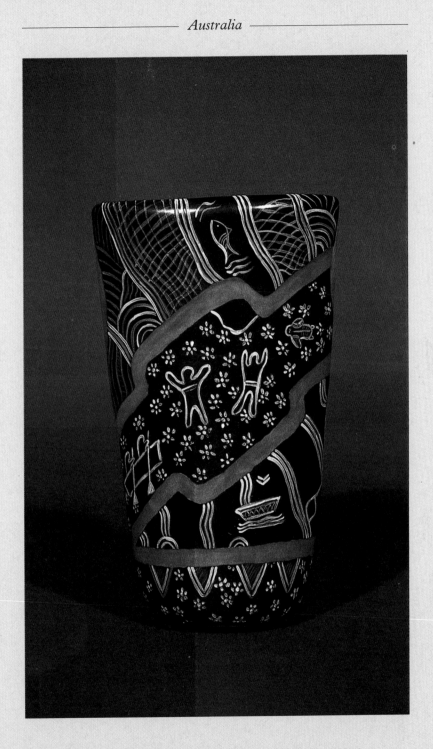

This large vase, based on aboriginal bark designs, has a black groundlay with raised paste decoration

There are no great porcelain factories in Australia's history, but the talents of contemporary porcelain artists more than make up for this. In my opinion, some of the finest hand-painted porcelain has been done by the china painters of Australia. There is no doubt that they are amongst the world leaders in our art. I think that one of the main reasons is that they are not afraid to experiment and develop new techniques. One only has to read the *Australian Porcelain Decorator* to realize that the whole continent is a hive of china painting activity, from the big cosmopolitan cities to the tiny mining towns miles from anywhere. Since the publication of my last book I have received letters from painters who in some cases are hundreds of miles from their nearest china painting centre, but who move heaven and earth to keep in touch. Surely the diversity of their talents must be connected with the fact that Australia is one great melting pot of cultures.

Apart from the wonderful climate of Australia two things stand out in my memory: first the warmth and hospitality of the Australian people, who certainly made this 'Sheila' feel welcome, and secondly the quality of light. After being used to the softly diffused light of the English climate I wasn't prepared for the bright, pure light which greeted our arrival in Sydney, and I had the distinct feeling that I had been living my life in a box with the lid on!

There is no doubt that, had I not gone to Australia in 1969 because of my husband's work, I would not be writing this book now. Thank you, Australia. You changed my whole life and I'm grateful. Perhaps one day I'll be back – who knows?

Aboriginal Designs

A wealth of mythology surrounds the Aborigines' Eternal Dreamtime – the time of creation. They are among the world's most ancient peoples, yet even after thirty-one thousand years of occupation in Australia relatively little is known of their history. Most of them today live in the Northern Territory, and the full-blooded Aborigine can speak both his own language and English. Through his dancing, singing, storytelling and art he depicts the history and mythology of his people – a most illuminating source of insight into their social organization.

I am including a few of the symbols represented in the Aboriginal art of the Eternal Dreamtime. These can be made into decorations for tiles to be set into tables, for vases and for large plates. The colours used are earth colours such as ochre, iron red, Sienna, umber and black.

Inspiration from Nature

I cannot discuss Australian art without a mention of the wild flowers to be found in the country. There is something magical about the flowers growing in the bush. Some of them are exceedingly bright and robust, such as the waratah. The flannel flower has to be seen (or felt) to be believed – the petals are the same texture as a flannel nightshirt, soft and downy white, with green-tipped petals and pale grey-green feathery foliage. It is not surprising, therefore, that so many Australian china painters love to paint their national flowers. Each state has its own floral emblem, which is often combined with the local fauna in their coats of arms.

I wanted to show one piece which was painted very many years ago by my teacher Elsie Flaxman, who lived at Roseville in Sydney, and who taught for several years in Chatswood. Unfortunately I do not own many of her pieces, but the flannel flower cup and saucer was sent to me by her daughter several years ago after Elsie had died, and is one of my most cherished possessions. She used a soft shade of Russian green for the flowers and foliage, and it was done in one firing.

I have included my own design of flannel flowers for you. It would look very nice wiped out of a green background or painted straight onto the white china. Note that the flower petals come to a graceful point at the end which is tipped with green; the centres are downy, soft and creamy white.

Aboriginal Project: Vase with Bark Painting Design

This vase was painted in a primitive style using typical Aboriginal designs. The centre panel symbolizes spirits travelling through the Milky Way and was copied from an authentic bark painting which I purchased in Australia. It was painted in Arnhem Land in the far north, and uses all the earth colours – black, brown, ochre, red. For the yellow designs over the black I used raised paste (for gold), as it was exactly the colour I wanted and showed up well in contrast to the black groundlaid background.

Royal Doulton teapot with Australian wild flowers
(Author's Collection)

Cup and saucer with flannel flowers, painted by the late
Elsie Flaxman

Flannel flowers on a plate

*A monochrome scene in New South Wales, painted over I F
satin metallic*

VASE WITH BARK PAINTING DESIGN

Colours used:
Deepest black, yellow raised paste, yellow-red

Number of fires:
As many as it needs to obtain the opaque, flat colours. I painted the vase one side at a time which needed about eight firings

Notes:
Choose the shape carefully for this style of painting – it must be simple, with no ornate scrolling etc. Paint a light design over dark, as the effect would be quite wrong with dark painted on light. The Aboriginal bark paintings are, of course, on wood, which is often stained to make the bark darker in colour

1st Fire
Mark out the areas which are to be red with masking fluid, and allow it to dry thoroughly. Groundlay the entire vase with black paint. Remove the masking fluid. Fire at 800°C.

2nd Fire
Paint the bands with yellow-red. You will probably need to do this two or three times to get a flat colour. Fire at 780°C.

3rd Fire
Mix up the raised paste thinner than you would if you were using it as a basis for gold. With a long brush, No. 2 or 3, apply the design. Fire at 760°C. You may do this a little at a time and fire it several times if you feel happier working this way. I did the entire side in one go, but the paste did need two applications to make it really stand out in contrast to the black.

Subsequent Fires
Sufficient to obtain the effect you wish.

Australian Flannel Flower

leaves are grey-green

pointed petals
tipped with
pale grey-green

Yellow wattle (acacia)

Gum (Eucalyptus)
Blossoms - there
are over 500
species

Gum nuts

Landscape Dish

This easy landscape was painted over a fired layer of satin metallic colour, which gives a beautiful glow to the piece. The metallic colour was one of the newer varieties which change colour as the light catches the surface – turn it this way and that and watch the colours change in an attractive, unusual way.

LANDSCAPE DISH

Colours used:
I F satin metallic yellow, dark brown

Number of fires:
Two

Notes:
Always wear a face mask when groundlaying with loose power. Fire the metallic colour very hot or it will not be permanent

1st Fire
Apply a groundlay over the entire surface with the metallic colour. Fire at 850°C.

2nd Fire
Paint the landscape dark brown, making the shading darker in the area nearest to you. In a landscape, the further away from you the paler the shading should be. Fire at 800°C.

9. United States of America

*The Statue of Liberty, a gift from the
French people to the United States*

In the USA there were a few porcelain companies in the eighteenth century but relatively little is known about them, and it was not until around 1826 that porcelain was produced in quantity. Notable factories were Weller, set up in 1850, Tucker (1825), Ott & Brewer (1863), Knowles, Taylor & Knowles (1872) and in 1880 the Rookwood factory. Then came the Lenox Company, founded in 1889 by Jonathon Coxon and Walter Scott Lenox. Lenox had been artistic director at Ott & Brewer, where he had learned the secret of making the lustrous porcelain called Belleek. Lenox now specializes in very thin decorative porcelain.

Painting on china, as an art form, has been popular in the USA since the end of the nineteenth century, and the Centennial Exhibition in 1875 seemed to be the catalyst. In no other country did enthusiasm for painting on china reach such proportions as in the USA, and in 1897, at the time of the first National Exhibition of Porcelain Painting in New York, it was estimated that there were ten thousand china painters in the United States.

Edward Lycett, who came from Staffordshire, stimulated interest in china painting from coast to coast and started a design business in New York, where his three sons also taught. Other painters of note at this time were the German Franz Aulich, who specialized in the painting of flowers and fruit, and the Austrian Franz Bischoff, whose specialities were roses and grapes. Vance Phillips, J. Stewart and Campana deserve a mention, too. Catherine Klein from Germany must also receive due credit for her wonderful flower and fruit watercolours, which are avidly sought by china painters all over the world.

With the two world wars, the difficulty of obtaining materials led to a decline in the hobby for many years. But in the mid-fifties trade strengthened and materials once again became available. Small groups formed and teachers were able to make contact for greater study. In 1960 the International Porcelain Art Teachers Inc. was founded by Lucretia Donnell Wideman as a forum for china painters. It has since grown into a truly international organization, with conventions and shows all over the USA. The World Organization of China Painters is also flourishing. Some of the porcelain painted by contemporary American artists is of the finest quality and destined to become the precious antiques of tomorrow. China painting is also extremely popular in South America, where beautiful designs are executed with great skill.

Feature Factory: Rookwood

The Rookwood factory was one of the most important in the history of American Art Pottery. It was founded in Cincinnati in 1880 by Maria Nichols with the help of her rich father Joseph Longworth, who was an enthusiastic patron of the arts. The factory was named after the family home. Mrs Nichols had done a little amateur ceramic decoration but the pottery was run on a commercial basis – although it did at first fire work painted by the Women's Pottery Club. Only decorative ware was produced, and one of the foremost painters was Albert R. Valentien. The pieces often reflected Japanese influence and for a while a Japanese artist, Kataro Shirayamadani, was employed. Rookwood pottery first attracted attention at the 1890 Paris Exposition where it won a gold medal. At the 1900 Exposition, Art Nouveau pieces were exhibited. Other factories imitated the Rookwood techniques but did not achieve the quality of the original.

One of the most popular techniques was one where lovely rich but muted effects were achieved in dark colours, and it is this one that modern china painters are mostly familiar with. This technique was developed by M. A. Daly with the use of an atomizer to apply colour, blending the reds, dark browns and orange under a glossy yellow glaze, and the colour scheme became associated with Rookwood's Standard ware. A new factory was built at Mount Adams in 1891 and floral decoration was frequent throughout the next ten years, but the subject matter also included portraits of American Indians, copies of Old Masters, animals and landscapes. Other artists of note were Laura Fry, Harriet Wenderoth and Fannie Auckland. At the end of the nineteenth century wall plaques were made and the pottery was extended to include an architectural department making tiles, mantelpieces, wall panels, fountains and exterior decorations.

Rookwood was at peak production from 1907 until 1913. The pottery closed briefly after financial failure in 1941 but reopened and resumed production by November of that year. During the American involvement in World War 2 part of the plant was used to make electrical parts and wooden pipes. From 1941 the pottery was owned by a scientific educational and research foundation under the jurisdiction of the Roman Catholic diocese of Cincinnati, and made various wares with a religious theme. In 1960 the company moved to Starkville, Mississippi, but the pottery ceased production in 1967.

The Rookwood factory began to use this monogram in 1886 with a single flame above it. Another flame was added each successive year until 1900

Rookwood Style Project: Chrysanthemum Plate

CHRYSANTHEMUM PLATE

Colours used:
Medium yellow, yellow-red

Number of fires:
Three

Notes:
Wear a face mask when groundlaying. For a really lovely
gloss on this project use bone china. Do not use
cadmium/selenium colours because they will fade. Test
fire your yellows and reds together first and find two that
are compatible

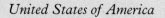

Chrysanthemums painted in a simplified Rookwood technique

Three Rookwood pieces: a vase with portrait of Chief Joseph of the Nez Percés; a ewer with dragon motif, marked with the initials of Albert R. Valentien; and a bowl with Japanese flower motif (Metropolitan Museum of Art, New York).
Photograph: The Bridgeman Art Library

Simple leaf design

Sheila Southwell

A design for a Rookwood style plate

1st Fire

Groundlay the plate with yellow, making sure that the whole ground is even and opaque. Fire at 800°C.

2nd Fire

With an ordinary black felt-tipped pen, draw your design on to the china. Using yellow-red and a flat shader, paint over the whole of the design completely with even strokes – you will still be able to see your design underneath. With a clean brush wipe out the chrysanthemum flowers and leaves, leaving plenty of strong highlights. Pad with silk the area where the red colour meets the yellow background, so that you do not get too sharp a line where one colours ends. Pad it almost out to the edge of the plate but not quite – you need some yellow around the edge. Fire at 800°C. The felt-pen lines will fire away.

3rd Fire

Mix a large quantity of yellow-red paint and cover the whole plate with this using a flat shader. Go over the entire plate with a silk pad, leaving a smooth layer of the yellow-red. You should see the strong yellow highlights left from the last fire quite easily. At this stage the design will look very rich. Fire at 800°C.

This technique is particularly suited to the painting of roses, leaves and scenery. Alternative colour combinations are pale blue and dark blue, pink and purple, pale green and dark green, pink and grey. On one of my seminars, the whole class painted the same subject using different colours and every one turned out beautifully. Remember you must groundlay the plate first with the PALER colour.

Patchwork China Box

Patchwork was introduced into America and Canada by English and Dutch settlers. As thrift and careful living was part of their rural life, most household linen and clothing was home-made. Mosaic patchwork became associated with quiltmaking, and elaborate designs were made up using scraps of odd material. Many of the designs have become traditional, and fine examples of this type of work may be seen in many museums. Some of these patterns, given such charming names as 'The Rocky Road to Kansas', 'Forest Path', 'Climbing Rose', 'Old Maids Ramble' and 'North Wind', are still worked today by needlewomen all over the world. In the early settlement days, quilting bees were popular: women gathered together to work with friends and neighbours on their patchwork. Often this was the only social contact these women had, as homesteads were miles apart. A dower chest was not considered to be complete without a bakers' dozen of quilts. The thirteenth was the bridal quilt, and at the quilting party held for it the marriage was announced. Patchwork designs are fun to do on porcelain. Why not get together at your next club meeting and hold a 'Patchwork on Porcelain' Bee?

PATCHWORK CHINA BOX

Colours used:
As many as you like

Number of fires:
Three

Notes:
Sketch lots of different designs on paper first, otherwise you will find yourself repeating the same pattern. Patchwork designs are suitable for vases, plates and tiles, which can then be mounted on ribbon to resemble a sampler

1st Fire
With a fine pen and black paint sketch the outline of the design on to the top of the box. Then pen the design on to the base. Fire at 780°C.

2nd Fire
Using any colours you like, paint the whole box. It would look lovely in different shades of one colour. Fire at 780°C.

3rd Fire
If necessary, add some more shading and fire again.

Patchwork Baby Design

A few suggestions
for your sections
of patchwork

frill detail

Sheila Southwell

China box with a patchwork design

Dogwood Dressing Table Set

Painting matching sets requires a little forethought. Assuming that the same flower is to be used on each piece, some consideration must be given to the various shapes and sizes of the porcelain. Do they complement each other in size and shape? It is a good idea to choose the largest piece first and then fit the others around it. Try to have an odd number of pieces – five is ideal. No one piece must be allowed to dominate the set when viewed together.

On some of the pieces you will see I have the design trailing down over the base from the lid. When doing this, make sure that the design fits together when the lid is in place. Always paint a tiny design inside your box and under the lid. This creates a nice surprise and gives extra appeal if you are painting the boxes for a gift. That little unexpected personal touch often pleases most. The dogwood blossom is a particular favourite of mine and is perfect for wipe-out techniques. It is the state flower of North Carolina and Virginia.

DOGWOOD DRESSING TABLE SET

Colours used:
Pale turquoise, chartreuse, moss green, yellow-brown, yellow-red, pansy purple, 22ct burnishing gold, white raised enamel, grey, black

Number of fires:
Three or four

Notes:
Suggested shapes include perfume bottles, lidded boxes, ring trees, candlesticks, pin trays and bells

1st Fire
Follow the same method on each piece. Paint with pansy purple where the main flower design is to be placed, gradually working outwards to include some pale turquoise and yellow-brown for a touch of warm colour. Using a fine toothpick or wipe-out tool indicate where the floral design is to be and then, with a turps-

Dogwood (Cornus) Blossom.

sheila Southwell

Dressing table set with dogwood blossom and raised enamel

The dogwood blossom in watercolour

cleaned brush, wipe the dogwood blossoms out of the background. Allow just a little of the colour to remain for shading. Wipe out the leaves and then paint in the stems. Fire at 800°C.

2nd Fire

Paint a wash of chartreuse over the leaves and add a little green to the flower petals – just enough to shade them delicately. Paint in the centres with moss green, forming the little round shapes as you go. Fire at 800°C.

3rd Fire

With a fine pen and using grey/black, faintly outline the flowers and the leaves, adding one or two 'shadow' leaves and blossoms. When the penwork is dry paint a wash of moss green mixed with pale turquoise over the shadow leaves and a wash of very pale pansy purple over the shadow flowers. This will 'push them into the background'. If the background needs any more colour, do it on this fire. Add a little yellow-brown to some of the leaves if the colours look too cold. Fire at 800°C.

4th Fire

With white raised enamel, finely outline some of the blossoms for highlights. Paint little dots of the enamel on the flower centres. With yellow-red and a fine brush paint the small frilled part of the petals. Paint any areas of gold. Fire at 760°C. Burnish the gold after firing.

Postscript

Well, here we are at the end of our journey around the world. I hope that you have found some styles and techniques to stimulate you to attempt something new, and that this book will help you to look at ceramics from other countries with a more enlightened view.

Index